Tabletop Vignettes

By Sharon Dlugosch

BRIGHTON PUBLICATIONS, INC.

BRIGHTON PUBLICATIONS, INC.

BRIGHTON PUBLICATIONS, INC.

PO Box 120706

St. Paul, MN 55112-0706

(612) 636-2220

First Edition: 1991

Library of Congress Cataloging-in-Publication Data

Dlugosch, Sharon

Tabletop Vignettes / by Sharon Dlugosch. — 1 st. ed.

p.   cm.

Includes index.

1. Business etiquette.   I. Title

TX871.D58 1991   91-39054

642' .8—dc20

ISBN 0-918420-16-4

Printed in the United States of America

A Note From the Author

This book came about because of my strong belief that one must have moments of beauty throughout the day to nourish the spirit. The everyday activity of eating can be one of those moments.

Eating for sustenance is an everyday necessity, but simply stuffing one's stomach isn't very soul satisfying. Experts say we spend 20 hours a week or 4 percent of each day in the act of eating. This time can be enriched by elevating the act of eating to the art of dining.

A book of tabletop vignettes fills a need to find small ways to add beauty to the act of eating, to make each meal a special occasion. In writing this book, I was reminded of many happy occasions of my first dinner party, of the baby's high chair pulled up to the dining table each evening, of the dining table set the night before, ready for the next evening's meal.

But more importantly, I set out to present a collection of tabletop ideas with enough variety to appeal to everyone's individual taste.

Tabletop Vignettes is organized into sections. The first section, "Dining Moments," deals with everyday meals. There you will find tabletop ideas to use throughout the day, including once-in-a-while afternoon teas, picnics, and dinners for two.

The next section presents a more whimsical look at table setting. Each theme is meant to create a picture or a mood for the table. You can dine European style or in old-fashioned comfort, with plenty of selections in between.

The seasonal selections can be used to help celebrate the holidays or a special time of year. Marking the passage of time through the yearly calendar gives a sense of order and ritual to our lives. Each theme reflects a particular time of year and makes use of seasonal foods and accessories.

There are times when a planned menu speaks to the table setting. In this section, the tabletop setting evolves naturally from the particular character of the menu. Sometimes special serving dishes are needed, or the menu may suggest certain ethnic table settings. The ideas found here will help you create a table to set off that special menu.

What special occasion or celebration doesn't revolve around

dining? To help you celebrate in style, there are suggestions for several major occasions. Most ideas can be used for any celebration with a little alteration to fit the party you have in mind.

In addition there are themes designed for special life-styles and situations. It is possible to dine elegantly in cramped spaces and with limited resources. You'll find suggestions that will help you perform magic with your table.

Finally you'll find a how-to section. The pragmatic and resourceful ideas in this section will give you the nuts and bolts of setting a special table — time after time.

Vignette in this case means "a sketch or picture." I hope that these sketches will inspire you to create beauty for yourself. After you read this book, I think you'll agree that any time you take time to eat, it's easy to take the opportunity to nourish your spirit as well. Start living a more beautiful life by creating lovely tabletop settings.

Contents

Dining Moments

Breakfast

You'll enjoy the first meal of the day if you make it easy and to the point: a cheery eye opener with quick but important table-top detailing.

Whether dining alone, eating in shifts, or enjoying a family-style sit-down, breakfast can be a soul-satisfying ritual. Organization and a touch of whimsy are key ingredients.

Since every minute counts in the morning, plan your space and time carefully. Organize your cupboards so there is a designated space just for breakfast supplies. Store a condiment tray of toppings for toast, cereal, and pancakes, as well as salt and pepper. The tray should be light and the size convenient so that it can be easily lifted out of the cupboard and then returned after breakfast.

In the same cupboard area, reserve space for place mats and napkins. Purchase or make fabric place mats in a color or print that appeals to you. A fabric place mat allows you to roll each place setting of mat, napkin, and flatware together and store it until the next morning, when it will take you just seconds to unroll and set the table.

A place mat with a pocket to hold the flatware is handy and easy to sew. A few stitches around the pocket and edges of the place mat are all that is necessary. For sewing and cutting instructions, see Sewing Table Linens in the "How-to Basics" chapter. To keep the first meal easy, use tableware that is dishwasher safe. After breakfast, pop the dishes in the dishwasher to be washed at a more convenient time.

Make sure the same favorite cups or mugs are available for yourself and each family member. Somehow a familiar cup every morning gives the same solace as the security blanket that comforts a child. Choose cups or mugs with funny sayings that speak to each owner. Cheerful colors and prints are another option.

Keep the centerpiece simple, but change it every so often to keep the table interesting. Some mornings tuck parsley sprigs in small juice glasses or egg cups for individual centerpieces. Other mornings place a colorful bowl of oranges, apples, and bananas in the center of the table. On another morning, write one-line love notes or special wishes for the day and tuck between the tines of the forks.

On dark winter mornings, place a potted amaryllis bulb on the table. This amazing plant will seem to grow before your eyes. Every day you'll see a distinct difference in its height, a warm and encouraging sight on a cold winter day.

Other Possibilities

- Pot perchers (little clay animals) start the morning off in a whimsical manner. Set these creatures clinging to the edge of cereal bowls or a fruit bowl centerpiece.

- Serve coffee European style. Europeans drink their morning coffee from cups that are larger than the cups most of us in the United States are used to. Their "coffee" is actually café au lait, a mixture of half coffee and half milk. Try it!

- Make a Mr. Potato Head game out of fresh fruit such as oranges. Put the plastic pieces on different pieces of fruit and display the funny fruit people in a shallow bowl.

- Set a toaster or waffle iron on the table for hands-on breakfast making. Old appliances have an appeal all their own. A 1920s or 1930s toaster that's almost a museum piece is surprisingly practical for toasting thick slices of homemade bread or sandwiches. It has two side panels that flip open to receive the bread. When one side is done, you turn the bread over to toast the other side.

- Tie a few festive, good-morning balloons on the backs or arms of the dining chairs to mark special family occasions or just for fun.

Brunch

Serve a leisurely-late morning meal. A display of well-designed appliances and a favorite cache of tableware pieces sets off this breakfast/lunch blend.

As you think through the brunch menu, you'll probably find that you'll need a variety of appliances as well as tableware to serve everyone smoothly. That means the serving table should be near an electrical outlet.

Any appliance or gadget on the serving table should be whistle clean. Some find that automobile chrome cleaners will polish up the well-used appliances in a jiffy. Of course, always check the cleaning directions of the appliance before using any cleaning agent.

Depending on your menu, you may need a toaster, waffle iron, griddle, blender, and warming trays within easy access by your guests. Provide an electric coffee pot or two, enough for two or three cups for each guest, and cups and saucers on a nearby separate table.

Pour the pancake or waffle batter into an earthenware pitcher, wrap bread slices in clean dish towels and put in a reed basket, and brown bacon or sausage and place them on a warming tray. You'll also need serving spoons and spatulas and pot holders. Since you'll be cooking on the serving table, use a stain-protected tablecloth.

Offer a selection of cold cereal at the serving table (two or three selections are enough). Pour each cereal into a serving bowl and place serving spoons nearby. Set a bowl that is large enough to hold a milk pitcher next to the cereal bowls. Spread a layer of ice on the bottom of the bowl. Place a dessert-sized plate upside-down over the ice and set the pitcher on top. Cover the top of the pitcher, except for the pouring lip, with plastic wrap to keep the milk fresh.

At the dining table, place baskets of sweet rolls, pitchers filled with juice, salt and pepper, butter, jam and jelly, and if needed, pancake and waffle toppings.

For each place setting, prepare a pleasantly arranged dish of sliced fruit and berries. Prepare the dishes the night before and store in the refrigerator. Then in the morning, at the latest possible moment set the chilled dishes on a dinner plate at each place setting. When your guests have finished with their juice and fruit, they may proceed with their plates to the buffet table.

Fruit in inexpensive glass dishes set on top of colorful dinner plates will set the ambience for this occasion. Color contrast the tablecloth and napkins to the plates. A medium-sized ceramic crowing rooster with a circlet of fresh daisies and smilax at its feet completes the setting.

Other Possibilities

- Any ceramic animal, such as a springtime rabbit, a mooing cow, a whimsical pig, or a quacking duck, will make a cheery centerpiece.

- If you enjoy handwork, cross-stitch a tablecloth and napkin set in a pattern expressly for the brunch table. This attention to the finer things in life will not be lost on your guests.

- Rather than prepared dishes of fruit, set a small plate with a fruit knife to the left of each place setting. Set a pedestal bowl of fresh fruit in the center for your guests' enjoyment.

- Decorate the handle of a reed basket with small silk flowers and ivy. Fill the basket with muffins, croissants, and fruit.

Lunch

Lunch implies a light, easy, and informal eating style. Although it's casual, it's important to spend time choosing tableware and linens that are sure to give a midday lift.

A casual soup-and-sandwich offering suggests a spirited and informal tabletop. You can achieve this contemporary style with a mix of modern plasticware and natural-fiber kitchen towels.

Set off place settings with crisp new cotton dish towels used as place mats. Fold the towel until it's about the size of a place mat and place on the table. Or turn the towel sideways and hang it over the edge of the table towards the lap. Select white towels with red, black, blue, green, or yellow stripes.

For dishes, use white or black plastic mini-trays for sandwiches and matching mugs for soup. You can find these in tabletop or import shops.

Complete the setting with casual flatware, either plastic handled or stainless steel. Lay a cotton napkin in a color matching the place mats to the left of the setting.

The centerpiece can be something as simple as a plastic pencil cup (white, black, or a color found in the place mats) filled with fresh Garbera daisies. Run a narrow towel, used for wiping glasses, down the center of the table.

A white-on-white textured look creates a different lunch look. Use white appointments, but vary the pattern and texture. Green and bright pink add attractive color accents to this setting.

Set white, eyelet-trimmed place mats on a tablecloth of bright pink-and-white plaid. Match the napkins to either the white place mats or the plaid tablecloth. Top the place settings with white stoneware dishes and sterling silver or stainless steel flatware. The serving dishes should be white, too.

Make a simple affair of the centerpiece by potting a trailing green ivy in a white, textured planter. The planter should have a self-saucer to keep moisture off the table. Otherwise, set the planter in a plastic saucer.

If practical, add cushions to the chairs around the luncheon table. Cover the cushions with plaid fabric that matches the fabric of the tablecloth.

Finally, consider a sun room or patio with lots of fresh air and sunshine as background for this luncheon setting.

Other Possibilities

🌿 Substitute paper napkins for the cotton napkins in an informal, contemporary setting.

🌿 Rather than a potted green ivy centerpiece, use a white teapot filled with pink, white, and lavender snapdragons.

🌿 For a rainy day luncheon, center a goldfish bowl or a large round goblet with two or three goldfish on the table. The gold of the fish and the red of a tomato-based soup will add bright color to an otherwise gloomy day. For fun, add goldfish-shaped crackers to the menu.

Teatime

The tea ritual. A small oasis of quiet time. Whether at home or at the office, this cherished repast offers an opportunity to display a lovely tea service and a collection of teacups.

A tea service is made up of teapot, creamer, sugar bowl, and, if fresh tea leaves are used, a tea strainer. It can be as informal as an everyday earthenware set, as stylish as a contemporary pottery design, or as elaborate as a beautiful silver display.

The tea service can be an exercise in nostalgia when it is a loving hand-me-down from parent or grandparent. Or it can be a happy reminder of a memorable trip. On the other hand, you could treat yourself to a new tea service chosen exactly for the setting in mind.

A formal tea, hosted at home is served on a large table. The tea service is set at one end of the table with a companion coffee or punch service at the other end. Dainty sandwiches, sweets, or cake are set on serving plates at the center. Serve oval domed shortbread cookies completely covered with powdered sugar, a favorite at teatime. These are often called Russian Tea Cakes, but they are also known as Mexican Wedding Cakes.

Cups and saucers are set around the tea service and the appropriate cups for the companion service at the other end of the table. Spoons are placed on or near the saucers. Plates, napkins, and flatware (if needed) are placed between the two services. Food on serving plates can be set above the plates but within easy-to-reach range.

Hosting a formal tea requires your best tea service and your loveliest table appointments. This is the time to use your best silver, china, and linens. Choose a centerpiece of fresh-cut or silk flowers.

The reverence for ritual carries over to the informal tea as well. The informal tea is usually taken in the living room. The tea service, cups and saucers, spoons, and napkins are brought in on a large tray and set on the coffee table. The plates and food are set near the tray.

Cover the tray with a white Battenburg lace cloth or a comparable linen piece. A collection of randomly acquired floral teacups and saucers strikes a lovely balance to this informal tea observance. Napkins that match or complement the Battenburg lace complete the setting.

Other Possibilities

🌿 Serve tea diluted with milk to the children in your life. Use child-sized tea sets made especially for children. Find inexpensive tea sets at the toy store or more costly ones in an antique shop. Invite a beloved teddy bear or a pretty doll to this affair.

🌿 Teatime offers a civilized break in a hectic office. A tea service can be quickly set up on a corner of a desk, If you're in an office where tap water isn't readily available, a hot/cold carafe can serve the same function as a teapot.

🌿 Any teatime setting will benefit from a single flower bud in a silver or crystal bud vase.

🌿 Sweet treats are an expected part of teatime. But, to be "veddy veddy" English, serve scones with clotted cream and jam.

🌿 If you've wondered about the strange-looking fabric doilie divided into several sections, it's a cozy for warm rolls or biscuits. Teatime is an occasion when you can use it. Set the fabric cozy in a silver dish.

Dinner at Eight

Tables like to dress up, too! As in fashion dressing, there are certain table setting guidelines to help you set a table with flair and panache.

A formal serving-at-eight occasion should have you reaching into your closet and storage centers for your best linens, tableware, and accessories. Elegant touches such as folded napkins, finger bowls, and name cards are other possible additions.

If you are doing the dinner without any serving help, it will be easier to serve buffet style. That is, set the serving dishes on a side table and let your guests help themselves. For dessert, clear the table and set dessert, dished out beforehand, at each place setting. Or simply serve dessert and coffee in the living room.

Before covering the dining table, lay a silence cloth on the top of the table. This is to muffle dining noises as well as to protect the table's surface. It also gives the tabletop setting a more luxurious look. Silence cloths can be purchased in a linen department or make do with something you have on hand. For example, use a thin blanket or mattress pad that fits your table. Always make sure the tablecloth adequately covers the silence pad.

A word about tablecloths: How you store tablecloths makes a difference in how much time you spend pressing out the wrinkles. (Of course, you're going to press out the wrinkles in the tablecloth before spreading it on the table.) Tablecloths of any size are best stored rolled around a tube. Use a large wrapping paper cardboard tube for this purpose. Large tablecloths will have to be folded lengthwise at least once before being rolled around the tube.

Another suggested storing method is to wrap a thick layer of tissue paper around a hanger, then hang the tablecloth over that. These storage methods save on the wear and tear of the tablecloths as well as preventing wrinkles.

Setting the table is a simple matter. Remember the basic rule of forks on the left, knives and spoons on the right. Place the utensils to be used first on the outside and work inward toward the plate. Place knives next to the plate. The water goblet is always above the tip of the knife and the salad or bread and butter plate is to the left of the dinner plate. Completely illustrated and detailed table setting and table serving suggestions are given in *Table Setting Guide,* available from Brighton Publications. See ordering information on page 144.

It's always correct to fold and place napkins to the left of the place setting. But napkins can add a great deal of flair to the table setting if they are turned into napkin sculptures and placed on the plate, to the left or above the plate, or tucked into glassware. For a variety of simple and fun folds see, *Folding Table Napkins,* Brighton Publications. See ordering information on page 144.

An attractive centerpiece completes the dinner table setting. Keep the centerpiece low so guests can have eye contact with one another or high enough so guests can see through the centerpiece. Also, the centerpiece should be of moderate size so it can be kept on the table throughout the dinner and still leave room for the serving dishes.

Other Possibilities

✿ Finger bowls, small bowls of water for rinsing fingers, are an important addition if the menu includes a sticky finger food. Set a small bowl of water garnished with a lemon slice above each place setting.

✿ Consider hiring one or two people to help serve and clean up after the dinner party. Having extra hands will give you more freedom to plan an elaborate menu and time to enjoy your guests during dinner.

✿ Name cards are a cordial and helpful addition if six or more people are attending the dinner party.

Dinner for Two

The focus shifts to a table set for two. This romantic, intimate setting is established with a light and dark color theme enhanced by sparkling accessories.

Dinner for two implies a medium to smallish table, but that is the only limitation. Whether it's a somewhat used kitchen table or a set-up-just-for-the-occasion card table, you can "costume" any table with linens. Of course, a finely wrought table gives you the choice of using fine place mats or tablecloths.

Cover the table with a black tablecloth large enough to drape over the sides at least 36 inches or until the edges just touch the floor.

Create a temporary scalloped hem as follows: Baste a straight line starting at the hem and running up the tablecloth about 3 to 4 inches.

Pull the thread tightly until you have the gathered effect you want, then knot the thread to fix it in place. Do this in as many places along the hem as you want. When you're tired of the scalloped look, simply take out the basting thread and iron the gathers out of the tablecloth. Other finishing touches for tablecloths can be found in the "How-to Basics" chapter.

At the point where the tablecloth is pulled up and caught, attach a large, glitzy ribbon bow. Choose a pink-tinged ribbon with a silvery cast. Tack it to the tablecloth with a basting stitch.

Set the table with white china, making a sharp contrast to the dark tablecloth. If the china is edged with a silver or black band, so much the better. Use your best crystal goblets and sterling silver or stainless steel flatware.

Accent each place setting with white or black napkins. Roll up each napkin like a scroll and tie a glitzy ribbon around it — the same ribbon you used for the pulled up points of the tablecloth.

Finish off in a bow.

A simple but romantic centerpiece can be fashioned from a jewelry box. Try to find one with a mirror fixed to the inside lid. Open the box so the mirrored lid is up and insert a small pot of ivy. The ivy vine should be long enough to trail out and around the box. The mirror will cast a reflection of the plant. Set the box to one side of the table so that both of you will see the front and a side of the box. Accent the box with casually draped silver beads. Set silver candlestick holders to the side and slightly behind the box. Use tapered white candles.

For the final touch, set a wine cooler on the table. Choose either plastic or glass. The night before, freeze flower petals and water in an ice cube tray. Rose, dendrobium, or hyacinth petals freeze well. Whole tea bud roses or mini-carnations can be used, too. Fill the cooler with the flower-filled ice cubes.

Other Possibilities

🌺 Change the accent beads and the candlesticks to brass.

🌺 Instead of using a black tablecloth, substitute a dark color such as eggplant or navy blue.

🌺 Stand a miniature art easel on the table to hold a written love poem.

🌺 Dress up old chairs or folding chairs by sewing covers for them in a color-coordinated print. Patterns are available in most major pattern catalogs.

Sunday Supper

Set out the pottery and terra cotta to accommodate a simple but hearty menu. A down-home look is just the thing for a warm, relaxing finale to the weekend.

Cover the table with a print cloth. The informality of a cotton print contributes to the casual spirit of a Sunday supper. A damask tablecloth is too formal for pottery and terra cotta pieces but a batik-inspired print or something like it, sets just the right tone for relaxed dining.

Set the table with oversized pottery plates — bowls, too, if the menu calls for them. Bright elementary colors and designs work well. The tablecloth and dinnerware should display the same unifying element, whether color or design.

Either old informal glassware that is interesting for its color or new chunky glassware can be used, both lend interest to the setting. If you're a collector, you may have an assortment of glassware. Sterling silver flatware will look out of place in this setting, so use informal stainless steel or plastic-handled flatware.

Select cotton and polyester napkins or loosely woven rayon and cotton napkins. When possible, match the napkins to the brightest color in the print. Place the folded napkins to the left of the plates or tuck the centers casually into the coffee mugs or glass goblets.

The centerpiece, in keeping with the style of the table, can be a simple arrangement of red, pink, orange, and yellow ranunculus. Fully opened roses or peonies are good alternatives. Tuck the flower arrangement into a terra cotta pitcher.

An assortment of fat, chunky candles is a good choice for the table. Put them in round terra cotta ashtrays. Select candles of the same color but in a variety of sizes. The table setting will look more interesting with the variety but will still be unified with color. Set the candles on the table in random groups of two or three.

Serving dishes can affect the success of the table, as well. Make an effort to slip in some whimsical elements. For example, fill medium-sized terra cotta flower pots with popcorn and crackers for a soup-and-sandwich menu. Or fill small terra cotta pots with shelled peanuts or carrot and celery sticks. Before using the pots, carefully wipe them out and tape over the drainage hole in the bottom.

Woven reed baskets have a rustic look that works well with pottery and terra cotta. Line the baskets with napkins, and use them for serving bread or rolls. Choose other serving pieces with the same casual and informal spirit — perhaps folk-motif tiles to serve as hot pads for the serving dishes. Serve coffee in a brightly colored thermal carafe.

Other Possibilities

- Envision a tablecloth and matching napkins in a happy vibrant plaid in sun-kissed colors.

- Skip the soup and fill the soup tureen with fresh flowers. Scatter a few blossoms on the table around the tureen.

- If the season is right, plant freshly cut tulips in terra cotta pots. Stick the cut stems in moistened florist foam.

- Create another easy centerpiece from annual flower boxes obtained from the local nursery. Stuff the boxes with favorite cut flowers.

- If serving a soup-and-sandwich menu, highlight the soup spoons. Use a different collectible soup spoon for each place setting or a set of soup spoons in a pattern that's different from the flatware.

A Great Ending

*Come for dessert! End the day with a
selection of sweet treats served, of course,
with minimum fuss but stylish savoir faire.*

When you've concocted an elegant dessert, you want to make
sure the presentation does justice to your creation. This special
dessert deserves to be set up in an elegant manner on the dining
table, the sideboard, or the coffee table. Use a handworked crochet
cloth or a square linen piece edged with lace as a tablecloth. Lay
out matching napkins.

A beautiful dessert deserves a beautiful serving dish. Use serving pieces that you wouldn't ordinarily associate with the dessert. In
other words, don't always use a cake tray to serve cake. A pedestal
cake tray, for example, can highlight individual tarts, cookies, or
fresh fruit and cheese.

In the same way, choose unexpected dishes for the individual
dessert servings. Serve pudding in crystal wine goblets or ice cream
sundaes in shrimp cocktail dishes . . . ice and all.

Serving utensils become important when you cut and serve the
dessert in front of your guests. There are many lovely pieces that fit
the occasion. The most elaborate are sterling silver or elegant crystal pieces. The "perfect" cake knife, pastry server, or berry spoon
should be items on your wish list. Confirmed antique and collectibles browsers may come across some wonderful finds. Those
who enjoyed a formal wedding can use the wedding cake knife for
other occasions.

Spirits are appropriate for some dessert settings. Arrange
decanters of dessert wines, sherry, and liqueurs, along with the
appropriate glasses, close to the dessert area. You'll also want to
use your best coffee server set for this elegant dessert setting.

A casual dessert and coffee occasion calls for a more relaxed
atmosphere. This dessert can be served from the kitchen counter as

well as the coffee table. Wherever you serve from, just do it with style.

A collection of dessert plates from vacation travels is a nice twist for serving dessert. Since they'll all be from different vacation spots, they'll give your guests a good ice-breaking start to the party.

Serve coffee in something a little different than the matching coffee mugs or cups from your dinnerware. Water glasses or glass cups with handles will give your dessert affair a slightly European flair.

Since this is a casual occasion, you will probably serve your guests in the living room. For their comfort and your furniture, offer "lapkins" instead of napkins to your guests. Lapkins are large-sized napkins that can be spread across and draped down from the lap. If you can't find them in stores, simply hem a 22- x 26-inch fabric piece to match or contrast with your dessert serving pieces.

Other Possibilities

- Stack fresh fruit on a tiered candy dish. Arrange the heavier, larger fruit on the lower tiers.

- Serve oven-warmed cheese in a fluted quiche dish. Use almonds to create a pattern or motif on top of the cheese.

- Acquire a set of eight 1950s-styled dessert and coffee plate trays. Shop for the all-in-one plates at a collectibles shop, or rummage through your parents' attic.

- To serve fresh fruit, use fruit knives styled with decorative enameled handles.

- When setting the table for an elegant dessert occasion, set a silver dish of sugar cubes topped with candied violets next to the coffee server.

Pampered Tray

You can almost always set aside at least one morning each week for lazy self-indulgence. Let the pampering begin with a set-just-right breakfast bed tray.

Prepare the breakfast tray the night before. Set out the tray, a cloth liner, a vase of flowers or objet d'art, and the tableware setting.

To extract the greatest satisfaction from this pampering ritual, plan the tray as carefully as you plan your attire during the week. The tray should be pleasing to the eye, and the food you prepare should be among your favorites.

The most important ingredient is the tray itself. It should be large enough to hold everything easily and steady so that it sits solidly on the bed or bedside table. Look in department stores, import shops, or mail-order catalogs for a bed tray that is just right for you.

Line the tray with a white linen cloth, perhaps a hand towel edged in lace or worked in a crochet pattern. Then set the tray with china from your best set or amuse yourself by selecting something whimsical.

The night before, pour the water into the coffee maker or teakettle so it only needs to be started in the morning. Some coffee makers can be preprogrammed to start at any time you desire. Take care of any tasks you can the night before, such as slicing lemons for the tea, chilling the melon pieces and berries, or pouring dry cereal into a bowl. Set any condiments you might need on the tray, too.

Consider what morning activity you're going to indulge in. If it's reading, select a good book or magazine the night before. Writing notes and letters? Set out the stationery and pen. Easy listening? Pick selections of your favorite music and have them at the ready.

Final preparations in the morning are simple. Pour the milk for the cereal into an amusing pitcher and add a single perfect flower to a crystal bud vase you've set out the night before.

Enjoy!

Other Possibilities

🦋 This is the moment to enjoy your hardly used silver tray and appointments.

🦋 Purchase an oriental lacquered tray with teapot, teacups, and saucers.

🦋 Buy brightly colored papier-maché trays with at least 1-inch sides. Use matching paper plates.

🦋 Bed trays are convenient as well as good looking. The sides straddle you in bed, and the side pockets are a special asset for holding books, magazines, or writing materials.

🦋 White wicker bed trays can be purchased in home-and-patio departments and shops or purchased through selected catalogs.

Picnic Delight

Strictly speaking, picnics are casual, out-of-door affairs. But who's to say this lighthearted repast can't be improved with the addition of a little indoor elegance.

Most picnics are a pleasant way to pass a few hours, but a picnic presented with flair elevates the occasion to a memorable moment. Using a few elegant components as well as one or two unexpected visual surprises is a good way to enrich the picnicking experience.

Because the picnic needs to be portable, careful advance planning is necessary to ensure success. Any extras will be too much to carry. Not enough, and you'll be without something you'll need. So your first step must be to decide where the picnic will be. Then you can find out what facilities and equipment will be available and can make your plans accordingly.

If tables aren't available, plan to picnic on the ground. Straw beach mats are hardy and attractive and provide a solid base for the picnic appointments.

Another workable idea is to dress the picnic spot with a floral tablecloth. It brings a little more indoor atmosphere to the setting. Pad the ground with a heavy blanket first to cushion the setting; then spread the tablecloth over the blanket. Low canvas chairs or slat-back wooden chairs grouped around the tablecloth are possibilities if the group is small. If the crowd is large, it will be easier to give everyone a small rag rug. Let the guests lounge near the tablecloth or wander off to rest their backs against a tree.

A wonderful visual way to demarcate the picnic site is to stake out the area with banners. Four or five colorful banners flying a hello in the breeze signals out-of-the-ordinary festivities for your guests. Cut banners out of hard-wearing duck cloth in bright colors taken from the floral tablecloth. Hem one end of the banners and attach them to 6-to-8-foot dowels. Glue or staple the fabric to the dowels. Stick the dowels in the ground at an angle.

Set your outdoor "table" with your best dinnerware to emphasize the elegance of this picnic theme. Use your best china. Roll fabric napkins around the sterling silver and tie the rolls with satin ribbon. Stick a flower in each knot.

Champagne served in stemmed glasses is part of the picture. If you don't have enough, rent some. You'll need to rent silver ice buckets, too, to keep the champagne chilled in an elegant manner.

Last, but not least, set a floral centerpiece in the middle of the "table," chosen to coordinate with the setting. Keep the flowers and container low and squat so the centerpiece won't tip in gusty winds. As an added measure, weight the vase with pebbles.

Many classic picnic baskets are available for carrying everything to the site in style. A good low-budget idea, especially if you have a great deal to carry, is to use decorator storage boxes. You can find pretty, floral print, closet storage boxes in notions departments. These boxes are made of lightweight cardboard and are slotted on the sides for easy carrying. After the picnic, use the boxes to store your off-season clothes.

Other Possibilities

- Picnic baskets with a place for everything are available in many gourmet and gift stores. Sometimes antique baskets can be found in antique or secondhand stores.

- For large crowds it may be easier to work with paper plates, tablecloth, and napkins in coordinated sets. The best part about paper products is they can be disposed of at the picnic site. No dirty dishes to carry home.

- You can create a more casual but still colorful setting with sturdy plastic dinnerware in scintillating colors.

- Palmetto fans, one for each guest, offer a languid and elegant way to keep cool.

Brown Bag Special

Brown bagging it for lunch doesn't always have to mean a dull, get-it-over-with-quick affair. An elegant lunch bag lifts the ordinary workday lunch to new heights.

Carry your lunch in a bag that is bright, attractive, and pleasing to you. Today you can find plain or print lunch-sized bags at greeting card shops or party supply stores in any color you can imagine. Miniature shopping bags are available, too. Their handles make them practical as well as attractive.

If you're ecology minded, you may want a reuseable lunch bag. Consider a fabric lunch bag. You can easily make your own with one-half yard of fabric and some cording. Choose fabric that is appealing to you and will give you a lift each time you handle the bag. This is one time you can indulge your taste for bright colors. A 100 percent nylon fabric offers brilliant color and is washable.

Cut out a 30-inch-diameter circle and sew a ¹/₂-inch-wide hem, either by hand or machine. Draw the cording through the channel of the hem. Leave 1 inch of the seam open so that you can slip the cording through the hole. To close, backstitch 1 inch on each side of the opening. To prevent the cording from slipping through the opening. tie a knot on each end of the cording and sew a button on each knot. The buttons — designer buttons or plain — should be large enough so they can't slip through the opening.

Package your lunch attractively. Use either blue or rose plastic wrap, rather than clear, to wrap your sandwiches and raw vegies. Put soup in a colorful thermos, and use pretty plastic ware for sliced fruit, salads, or puddings.

Tuck a water glass instead of a plastic cup into the lunch bag to hold cold beverages. For hot beverages, wrap an elegant china cup and saucer or a colorful ceramic mug in the napkin and pack it in the bag. Rather than taking a cup and saucer from your complete set, look in antique or collectible shops for a single cup and saucer that catches your eye. Then you won't have to worry about breakage and replacement.

Choose a napkin that is color-coordinated to the lunch bag. Use a plain, colored fabric for the lunch bag and a coordinating striped fabric for the napkin. So you won't be tempted to use plain paper napkins, select wash-and-wear fabric for easy care.

The well-equipped lunch bag includes a centerpiece for the place setting. Something small but eye-catching, like an energizing amethyst crystal or a silk posey, will measurably increase your luncheon pleasure.

Other Possibilities

🌸 If you have a scrap of fabric left over from sewing the lunch bag, make a small sachet-sized bag. Just large enough to hold change, the sachet bag will ensure that you will have coins on hand for the beverage dispenser.

🌸 Bring along a pleasant lunchtime companion . . . such as a recently received letter from a friend. Read and enjoy as you're eating lunch.

🌸 A steady diet of anything will eventually dull the senses, so make it a point to change the lunch bag and accessories periodically. It's important to feed your eyes as well as your stomach.

🌸 A personalized lunch bag makes a lovely present for the working woman who enjoys the finer things in life.

Table Styles

French Impressions
Fruitful Design
Painted Fantasy
Eastern Flavor
Handcrafted Artistry
Homespun Setting
Old-fashioned Charm
Enchanted Whimsy
Kid Stuff
European Appeal
Table That Memory

French Impressions

Create an Impressionistic table setting inspired by a Monet-like garden. Light-splashed colors and floral prints intensify the French countryside theme.

The interesting thing about this table setting is that it uses neither tablecloth nor place mats. Set the table appointments on an uncovered, well-cared-for tabletop. Eighteenth-century, classic-styled table and chairs offer a wonderful Continental background for this table setting.

The use of floral plates at each place setting imparts a flower garden look to the table. There are any number of floral patterns to choose from in both china and casual ware. You'll find dinnerware with decorative borders of tiny flowers, large blossoms planted overall, and everything in between.

Lend a classic flavor to the table with the flatware design. You'll find a variety of country French designs in sterling silver, silverplate, and stainless steel.

White napkins (either cotton/polyester or linen) edged with lace should accent the place settings. Pull each napkin through a porcelain napkin ring decorated with a painted porcelain flower.

Grace the center of the table with floral topiaries. Ask your florist to make up two topiary balls covered with pink and yellow roses. Stand them in terra cotta flower pots. Cover the tops of the pot with moss. Center the pots on the table. As if by accident, drop one or two fresh roses on the table near the pots.

Repeat the rose floral motif by mounding pink and yellow roses in tiny terra cotta pots. Plug the hole at the bottom of the pots with florist clay before filling with water. Set the pots on a liner to prevent the moisture from seeping through onto the table. Place a pot above the forks at each place setting, or set one pot between two place settings.

Wooden turned candlesticks set at random in the center of the table add more charm to the table. Keep the height of the tallest candlestick lower than the topiaries. Use cream-colored candles.

To further advance the illusion of a garden setting, place wicker baskets of garden flowers around and about the dining area. The rustic texture of the baskets charmingly accents this Impressionistic table setting.

Other Possibilities

- Monet prints on the walls of the dining area add richness and authenticity to the French flavor of this setting.

- Instead of pink-and-yellow-rose topiaries, substitute fresh green smilax or ivy. The plant you choose should have lasting quality so that it will still look fresh after several hours.

- If your tabletop is less than desirable, cover it with a bright yellow tablecloth. Yellow tablecloths were often used in the Monet household.

Fruitful Design

Enjoy the freshness of fruit represented in the world of tabletop appointments. Whether painted, stitched, or scuplted, the fruit motif is a cheerful addition to any tabletop.

To make the place mats and napkins for this table setting, select a white or ivory cross-stitch fabric. Before cross-stitching, finish the edges with a simple rolled hem, slip-stitched in place. A slip stitch is simply a hemming stitch in which the needle is inserted through the folded part of the hem and a few threads of fabric are picked up on the inside so as to be invisible on the outside.

There are many sources in which to find fruit patterns for your cross-stitch project. You may want to select one kind of fruit, such as apples, or work out a variety of patterns, such as grapes, pears, plums, and so on. The sumptuous fruit motif is featured in many cross-stitch sets.

Complement the cross-stitch place mats with a centerpiece of assorted fruits. Soft fabric sculpture, wood, glass, and papier-maché are just a few of the three-dimensional fruits available. The best thing about this type of fruit is that it will always appear fresh.

Arrange a filmy gauze runner in the bowl, with the fruit nestled on top. Allow one end of the gauze runner to drape from the side of the bowl and down along the table. The color of the gauze should provide a contrast to the fruit arrangement while blending with the cross-stitch place mats and napkins.

Any basic white, ivory, or luster china coordinated with the place mats is lovely. A plain border on the dinnerware is good, but a border of fruit or fruit blossoms intensifies the fruit theme.

Choose clear glassware, tinted lightly green, to make a sparkling fresh statement next to the dinnerware. The same tinted green glass for candlestick holders and water pitcher adds balance to the table setting.

Try to find one or two ceramic accessories that feature the same fruit motif as you've chosen for the table linen. Collectibles shops, wholesale outlets, and fine tableware shops are all possible sources. Consider serving dishes, a pitcher, or perhaps salt and pepper shakers decorated with the fruit motif you've selected.

This setting won't be complete without at least one piece of majolica. Majolica (pronounced mə jäl´i kə), is 19th-century pottery embellished with ornate sculptural modeling of fruits, flowers, birds, and other animals. It is prized for its jewel-like colors. Antique majolica plates, bowls, vases, and serving pieces are enjoying a revival. Consequently, you can find many relatively inexpensive reproductions today.

Other Possibilities

🍂 Choose napkin rings with a fruit motif, either sculptural or with a painted design to hold napkins in place.

🍂 Reproductions of porcelain boxes originally used for snuff are making a comeback. These porcelain boxes, crafted to represent apples, peaches, and other fruits can be used as accent pieces on the table.

🍂 Look for glass serving dishes decorated with a raised fruit design. Some have an applied radiant color, that adds sparkle to the tabletop.

🍂 Fresh lemon slices in water glasses enhance the fruit motif theme.

🍂 Pick the dessert to coordinate with the motif: Strawberry? Choose strawberry shortcake. Raspberry? Choose fruit compote. Pineapple? Choose pineapple upside-down cake. Set the dessert in the center of the table.

Painted Fantasy

Beguile the eye with decorative painting.  *A fantasy finish can beautifully decorate the tabletop or highlight individual tableware pieces.*

Jazz up a plain wooden table with place mats painted on the tabletop. As a camouflage for a scarred tabletop or as sheer whimsy, faux place mats take table setting to new heights.

You may choose to use a "trompe l'oeil" literally meaning "fool the eye" finish to fix a permanent runner and place mats on your table. The trompe l'oeil finish is a two-dimensional painting that creates the illusion of a three-dimensional object. Reference books readily available in bookstores and libraries, can tell you more about how to apply this finish. Since this process demands a certain expertise, you may decide to commission an artist to create the effect you're after.

Stenciling, on the other hand, requires less skill. Simply design and cut a stencil pattern and paint. Repeat the stencil pattern as many times as you want. For place mats, cut one stencil and use it at each place setting. For the runner in the middle of the table, use an extended version of the place mat stencil pattern. Stencil how-tos are discussed in the "How-to Basics" chapter.

With either the trompe l'oeil or the stenciling technique, select colors that will compliment your table appointments and the dining area decor. If you are at a loss for a design, you can "borrow" the design from your dinnerware.

If your dinnerware design doesn't inspire you, paint a simple border of ribbons and flowers with a floral cluster bouquet in the center. Otherwise purchase a stencil. There are many stencil designs that you can adapt for use if designing your own pattern is too much of a challenge.

You can use a paint marker or brush paint on clear glass votive lights in the same style as the place mats. Consult a craft store about enamel paint that will work on glass. Set white or color-coordinated candles in the glass votive holders.

Your painted fantasy will give you a beautiful, perpetually dressed table to give you pleasure throughout the day. When you want to change your tabletop decor, simply lay a tablecloth over the table and build a completely new look for the occasion.

Other Possibilities

🍂 Design your painted tabletop from a favorite whimsical pitcher. After painting the faux place mats, paint a round design on the center of the table as a place of honor for the pitcher.

🍂 Choose a design to blend with the period of your dining area. For example, to match country furnishings, use country motifs and colors.

🍂 For the trompe l'oeil finish, you may want to paint realistic-looking dinnerware and napkins on the place mats as well.

🍂 Hide imperfections in the table with a strategically planned, painted design.

🍂 Stencil fabric place mats and napkins. The best fabric for stenciling is plain cotton. Hand wash gently or use the delicate fabric cycle.

🍂 Stencil a corner of a plain napkin, copying just a small portion from the tablecloth or table design.

Eastern Flavor

Savor the dramatic essence of the Far East. Let the print of the table linen and the glow of the brass appointments hint of the richness of the anticipated dining experience.

Cover the table with a rich paisley print tablecloth of wine red, deep green, and cream. Some fabrics have a gold pattern stamped on the print. You may find this special tablecloth at tabletop shops or in linen departments. Otherwise, look for fabric similar to the paisley print at fabric shops or import shops. Sometimes bed sheets from the linen department prove a surprising and inexpensive fabric find. For information about how much yardage is required for napkins, place mats, or tablecloths see the "How-to Basics" chapter.

Poufing the tablecloth at each corner gives a soft swag to the sides of the tablecloth. When you lay the cloth on the table, gather up a little of the tablecloth at each corner to create a decorative pouf. You'll need four brass cafe curtain rings, one in each corner, to keep the poufs in place. Simply gather up fabric at one corner of the table, and pull it through the ring until you have a pouf large enough not to slip back through the ring. Pull the fabric in such a way that the poufs stand up and out at each corner.

Now continue to set the table. When building a place setting, keep the menu in mind. Be aware of what dishes you'll need for each course. In this setting, start with a large flat brass plate to be used as a charger for the dinner plate. The brass charger should be at least ½ to 1 inch larger in diameter than the dinner plate. Then, on top of the dinner plate, place a salad plate and a napkin folded in the shape of a rose. Choose a napkin at least 16 inches square. A wine red fabric will complement the red in the tablecloth and provide a jewel-like color base for a white lotus cup placed within the napkin folds. You may want to serve something like a broth-based soup in the lotus cup.

The rose fold liner is made in this way: Open the square napkin and lay it flat, with the right side facing down on the plate. Fold the four corners (points) to the center, and again fold four points to the center. Turn the square over face down on the plate. Again, fold four points to the center. If you're right-handed, hold down the points in the center with your left hand and, reaching underneath to grasp a point, pull out the first rose petal. After pulling the point up, coax it a little so it leans a bit toward the center. This takes a little practice, but once you've gotten the hang of it, it's very simple. Repeat with all the points. Then reach underneath the sides and pull out the leaves of the rose. All the time you are doing this, you should be holding the center points down tight. Mold the rose petals and leaves with your right hand while holding tight to the center points. Place the lotus cup in the center of the rose. The Rose Fold directions, illustrations, and photo can be found in *Folding Table Napkins,* available from Brighton Publications.

At the side of the place setting, to left of the forks, place a napkin that is of the same fabric as the tablecloth. Casually pull the center of the napkin through an open-work, brass napkin ring.

In the center of the table, place a bamboo cricket cage (a bamboo bird cage may be easier to find), with green vines spilling from it onto the table. Then march a trio of brass or papier-maché elephants around the cage with trunks held high, signifying good fortune. An import shop is the best place to find the elephants.

Around the centerpiece and between the place settings, set brass candlestick holders. Collect all styles and sizes: slender tapered candles, chunky pillars, votive candles. Keep consistency by using candles of the same color; off-white works best.

Other Possibilities

* If you can't find a bamboo cage, set a green vine plant in a filigree brass box to use for your centerpiece, for another exotic look.

* Any brass accessory such as wine goblets or trivets for serving dishes will give an added gleam to the setting.

* Instead of brass rings use grosgrain ribbon bows to hold the tablecloth poufs in place.

Handcrafted Artistry

In an age when machine-made items are the norm, one-of-a-kind crafts are stylishly setting new trends. The use of handcrafted, individualized beauty increases dining pleasure.

Working with elemental materials as wood, clay, glass, and fabric, today's artisans are producing visually pleasing pieces handcrafted for the dining room. Although a complete handcrafted table setting may not be within your reach now, one or two loved objects can lend a personalized artistry to the table. And you can acquire unique new pieces through the years.

The table and chairs themselves can be one-of-a-kind statements. Look for furniture with hand-hewn embellishments or furniture that is witty or tongue-in-cheek. When commonplace objects are made ornate and decorative, people slow down to notice them and, in pausing, their eyes are often opened to the potential for beauty and humor all around them.

Handcrafted table linens are available in a wide range of craft interpretations. A jewel-toned ikat runner or a handwoven chimayo-style runner can decorate the table. If you prefer, you can cover your table with a hand-painted tablecloth or a linen tablecloth edged in hand crochet. Hand-woven place mats and napkins create a wonderful textural background for the solid style of some pottery dinnerware.

Dining with handcrafted art is like living with "art" as family. Using handcrafted dinnerware pairs the commonplace activity of eating with a pleasurable visual experience but without the sense of being in a museum. Such choices as multihued earthenware dishes, pottery dinnerware edged with gold, or fluted porcelain plates and bowls make a sensual dining experience possible. Handcrafted dinnerware can be traditional, exemplifying accepted plate and bowl forms, or it can be free-form motifs in variegated colors. Always make your choice in view of what is most appealing and satisfying to you.

The art of dining well includes the flatware as well. Hand-hammered utensils and futuristic sterling silver often make definitive statements with their distinctive forms. On the other hand, some artists fuse brilliant color to anodized aluminum and stainless steel flatware.

Anodized aluminum is also being used to craft goblets, sometimes with brass or other trim. Handblown glass is visually intriguing, with its handsome form and color. Goblets delicate and etheral or chunky and solid are always a sensory and visual experience.

If you have only one or two handcrafted objects, put them to use in the table setting. Hand-thrown ceramic platters, quilt-patterned terra cotta serving plates, or sculptured porcelain vases can lift your table to a state of art.

A precarious balancing act begins when you set the table with part economy dinnerware and part handcrafted pieces. This is the time to observe the principle of weights. Although the materials may be different, use the same weight of materials for all the pieces. For example, mixing pottery and lightweight plastic is generally not desirable. On the other hand, blending colorful earthenware pieces such as Fiestaware™ with a few chosen pieces of pottery can create a successfully balanced table setting. Use the economy pieces as background and display one or two handcrafted pieces as the focal point or showpiece.

When shopping for handcrafted items, remember they are personal, and even when produced in quantity, unique. The not-quite-straight angle of the chair, the slight imperfection in the glass or fabric signals the craftperson's distinctive work. Anything made by hand will always be more expensive but will truly be well worth the price.

Other Possibilities

🌸 Raku blends well with brown-tone economy stoneware. Raku is a low-temperature fired pottery and often has a metal oxidized glaze such as a copper oxide finish. Complement the copper oxidize glaze by adding a copper vase or copper napkin rings to the table setting.

Homespun Setting

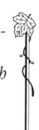

Summon visions of a simpler and plainer time. A down-home country look spotlights this table; letting you mix-and-match homespun hand-me-downs.

Braided rag rugs laid across a maple or pine trestle table forms the background for this setting. Lay small scatter rugs across the table allowing the tabletop to show between the rugs. Set a place setting on each end of the rug. If your table has a less-than-wonderful top, then cover the entire tabletop with rugs. Place the rugs side-by-side diagonally on the table.

Accent the rugs with coarsely woven napkins, either all cotton or a cotton/rayon blend. The color intensity of the napkins should be a step up of the predominant color of the rugs.

Grandmother's bean pot will provide continuity to this theme. Fill the pot with seasonal plants. For example, the summer season suggests a full blooming geranium plant for the bean pot. Tuck asparagus ferns around the edges of the pot. In the fall, use chrysanthemums; in winter, use forced tulip and daffodil bulbs.

In keeping with the simple and plain look, use everyday pottery or ironstone dishes. Add an unexpected touch to the place setting with pint-sized canning jars. The wide-mouth ones are best. If you are rummaging through boxes of jars, look first for the blue-green glass kind.

Besides having fun using these jars as glasses, you'll find them to be practical as well. You can pour any beverage, hot or cold into them. Garnishes of mint leaves or a thin lemon slice add color and style to a cold beverage.

Serving containers offer another opportunity to emphasize the homespun look. Wrap hot biscuits or corn bread in an old-fashioned white square dish towel, the kind that is embroidered in one corner. Serve coffee from a stove-top coffee pot and cold beverages from a clear glass pitcher. Search your cupboards for odds and ends to use as serving pieces for the rest of the meal.

Mix-and-match chairs give an added appeal to this setting. You can pull up benches, a rocking chair, or any odd chair to this table setting. In "making do," you'll be right in style!

Consider room accents to help you pull together this theme. An old copper boiler can be set next to the fireplace and filled with wood or put into a sunny spot and stuffed with potted green plants. Show off a collection of china nesting hens on a wall shelf and lean a washboard on a chair by the entrance to your dining room. Hand write the menu in large script on a ruled piece of paper and tack it to the washboard.

Other Possibilities

🐾 Plastic-handled flatware though contemporary, still complements this homespun setting.

🐾 Instead of pottery dinner plates, use your accumulation of tin pie plates for the same purpose.

🐾 Placing a kerosene lamp in the center of the table can serve as centerpiece and light source. In the evening it will cast its soft romantic light on the table.

🐾 If you're desperate for more tables to accommodate guests, simply haul in a wooden picnic table and benches or place planks across wooden or metal carpenter horses. Then cover the table completely with rag rugs and go on from there.

Old-fashioned Charm

Borrow from yesterday for nostalgic charm. Soft white or pastel colors, old dishes from Grandma's cupboard, and a few handicraft pieces lend a warm, soothing touch to the dining experience.

Either a prized round pedestal oak table or any country-style kitchen table will serve this charming ensemble well. Select a favorite color in a narrow stripe fabric to cover a plain table, cut a round piece of fabric the circumference of the table plus the floor length from two lengths of fabric sewn together. Cut out a smaller piece for a oak table to show off the pedestal. See the "How-to Basics" chapter for cutting and sewing round tablecloths.

To finish the hem of the tablecloth, fuse a border of fabric roses around the hem. When you purchase the striped fabric, select a rose-print fabric in complementary colors. The roses in the print should be clearly defined and somewhat uniform in size so they can be cut out and applied evenly around the hem. To determine the number of roses you will need, measure the width of one rose. Divide the total inches of the hem by that number. For complete directions, see the Easy Appliqué Method in the "How-to Basics" chapter. Roses fused to the edge give the tablecloth a scalloped look, eliminating the need for a finished hem.

When you've finished the tablecloth, start work on the napkins. Make 22-inch-square napkins out of the same striped fabric. Tablecloth and napkins should be a cotton or cotton blend, preferably with a stain-release finish. Finish off the napkins with a machine-sewn ¼-inch hem around all four sides.

To make napkin rings, cut 4 x 6-inch strips of striped fabric, fold each length in half, right sides together, and sew. Keep the ends open. Turn right side out and fuse one rose, the same size or smaller than the tablecloth roses, on the center of the ring. Sew the ends together.

If you still have sewing enthusiasm, complete the ensemble

with matching chair cushions. Using the same striped fabric, make ruffled cushions to fit the dining chairs. Sew a ruffle on three or four sides of the cushion, depending on the design of the chair. Leave a small space between the chair back and seat.

Set the table with a collection of Depression-style dishes. Depression dishes are clear glass dishes that were made in a variety of patterns and colors in the 1920s and 1930s. Because these dishes were popular and plentiful in their day, you may be lucky enough to find pieces squirreled away in a relative's cupboard. Barring such luck, you can probably find these dishes at antique and collector shows.

For the centerpiece, choose a white wicker flower pot or a ceramic pot made to look like wicker, and set a flowering hydrangea plant in the pot. Complete the look with a pressed glass pitcher filled with lemonade and set next to a plate of homemade sugar cookies.

Other Possibilities

- If you can't find a complete set of Depression ware, collect different styles or colors and make up a different pattern for each place setting. Or collect dinner plates in one pattern and salad plates in another.

- Inexpensive dinnerware from the 1940s once available in dimestores, make the same old-fashioned statement. Color-coordinate the tablecloth to the dinnerware pattern.

Enchanted Whimsy

Bits of whimsical delight, such as filmy fabric, shiny ribbon, and light-reflecting glassware, conspire to present a table of enchantment.

Purchase a length of white tulle (pronounced *tool*) from a fabric store. Buy enough so that the tulle length covers the center of the table. Finish off the ends with a machine- or hand-sewn hem. The selvage or side edges of the piece do not have to be hemmed.

Handling the tulle gently, tie the length into a large loose knot. The knot should be loose enough, yet solid enough, to form a solid round base in which you can set a vase of flowers. Drape the two ends of the tulle and let them fall lightly and naturally down the table.

Now you are ready to arrange the centerpiece. Find a tall, round, see-through glass vase and fill with white garden flowers. Choose a variety of flowers to give you a variation of blossom shapes. For example, white phlox, snapdragons, and tea roses are a good combination.

Before you place the bouquet in the vase, tie a wide white satin ribbon bow around the bouquet. Tie the stems in such a way that the ends of the stems form a fan. Tie the bow around the stems so that it is partially visible through the glass vase, but place the bow high enough that it is above water level.

On and about the tulle ends laying on the table, set small glass boxes of posies. Select white tea rose buds and baby's breath and fill three or four glass boxes. The night before, cut florist foam in a small square to fit each box, and soak. The next day, set the drained foam square in the glass box and arrange the tea roses and baby's breath. Keep the lid of the box in an opened, upright position.

If serving dinner, the addition of candlelight will add to this vision of light and grace. Simply place white votive candles in see-through glass roly polys. Then set the roly polys on small mirrored squares. Set as many candles as you have room for on the table.

You can experiment with several kinds of place mats, but you'll likely agree, Battenburg lace placemats give the most grace and quality to this table setting. Set white dinnerware with metallic or color bands, or choose white-on-white patterned dinnerware. Finish off the placesettings with sterling silver flatware and crystal goblets.

If using matching Battenburg napkins, roll them loosely and pull through napkin rings. As for the napkin rings, purchase or make tiny whitewashed vine wreaths. The wreaths should be small enough that they can be used for napkin rings. Entwine 1/8-inch satin ribbon around the ring and finish with a tiny bow, allowing the ends to fall loosely. Choose two ribbons, white and a color used in the dinnerware set. If your dinnerware colors are all neutral, choose white and hot pink or leaf-green satin ribbons.

Other Possibilities

- Fill a glass vase with white tulips. Tie the stems with a wide white bow. Then instead of the filled glass boxes, simply tie satin ribbon around a tulip and casually lay several of these one-stemmed bouquets around the table.

- In place of glass boxes for the small bouquets, use glass oil-and-vinegar cruets.

- Verdigris candleholders with white candles can substitute for the votive candles. These give a bit of color and extra height to the table.

Kid Stuff

Brighten kids' meals with a child-centered tabletop look. A child's possessions are the basis for creative linens, tableware, and centerpieces and extend the child's world to the dining experience.

A wealth of material for table use is as close as your child's bedroom or toy box. You can create a delightful table with just a few minutes of cutting, pasting, and arranging.

A child's handprint is an effective way to personalize tablecloth or place mats. Remember to add the date and the child's name so that it's noted and recorded for all to see.

Fusible web products easily and simply transfer handprints onto fabric. Trace the child's hand onto a square of fabric. Following the manufacturer's directions, simply iron the fusible web product to the underside of the hand-traced fabric. Then cut the outline of the hand out and peel off the special paper backing. Fuse the handprint to the tablecloth or the place mat. See the Easy Appliqué section in "How-to Basics" for more complete directions.

Before fusing the fabric handprint, write the child's name on the palm of the hand and date it across the wrist. Use either a felt-tip pen or work the name in the fabric with embroidery floss.

Child-patterned place mats can be made in a jiffy using leftover wallpaper from your child's bedroom or from wallpaper samples. Cut out two pieces of wallpaper the size of place mats (12 x 17 inches) and glue the undersides together. Laminate both sides of the place mat and finish off the edges by cutting inverted scallops. You'll find lamination material at office supply stores. These place mats are easy to clean and quick to make.

Little ones will be happy to supply you with their treasured collections or favorite toys for the table's centerpiece. Miniature cars, alphabet blocks, or plush animals can be used to set the theme of the table. Letting the children do the arranging of the centerpiece will increase their feeling of involvement.

Any time the child has received promotional items of favorite characters, such as mugs, pitchers, or plates, set up the child's place setting featuring the item. Child-sized tea sets and toy dinnerware sets can be used, too, and not just for the child's place setting. Bringing the adult's place setting down to the child's size is an interesting family togetherness experience.

There are other benefits in setting a table with kid stuff. For one, it can provide a daily learning experience for the child. Each week, emphasize something different, such as colors, the alphabet, numbers, or zoo and farm animals. For instance, make a point to set the table with each place mat a different color, or set a different miniature plastic animal at each place setting. While eating, compare one another's colors or animals.

Other Possibilities

🐾 Use the handprint-decorated tablecloth when Grandma and Grandpa come to dinner. When dinner is over, give them the tablecloth as a one-of-a-kind present.

🐾 Instead of laminating wallpaper for place mats, use the child's rainy-day art projects.

🐾 Characters from children's classics such as *Wind in the Willows* and *Alice in Wonderland* can inspire unique table settings.

🐾 Consider using terrycloth wash cloths as napkins. What could be more appropriate for young sticky hands?

European Appeal

Looking for a table setting to suggest a time of quiet elegance? Try a European look combining classic dining elements with the design influence of the Orient.

Underline the table setting with a blue-and-white chinoiserie (shēn´ wä zə re´, a Chinese style of decoration) print fabric. Often birds, trees, or flowers are featured in this print. The tablecloth should be long or large enough so that the hem brushes the floor.

Top this blue-and-white print fabric with a smaller square of white, lace-edged cotton or linen cloth. Lay the cloth so the four corners are hanging equidistant from the tabletop, about a 6-to-8-inch drop.

As you set the table, include both European and Oriental elements in the tabletop. Set the table with blue-and-white, Oriental-influenced, Willow pattern dinnerware. The Blue Willow pattern, a long-time favorite, is widely reproduced.

Set traditional-style flatware next to the plate, but lay the flatware in the Continental manner. Fork tines and the bowl of the spoon are in the usual place but are placed facing down on the table. Eating with the fork held in the left hand and knife in the right hand is Continental style.

In the same Continental manner, the water glass is placed at the top of the spoon and the wine glass is set back behind the water glass, rather than forward and closer to the edge of the table. Use stemmed goblets for this setting.

Highlight the Blue Willow dishes with white, lace-edged napkins intricately folded. The napkins should be large, square, and dinner sized (at least 22 inches).

The center of the table should display an Oriental design–influenced porcelain vase filled with garden flowers. Select blue or rose-violet flowers such as asters, phlox, or delphiniums. Arrange the flowers in a loose style in the European manner.

Set a candlestick lamp on each side of the vase. Candlestick lamps are tall candlestick holders and candles with lampshades set above the candles. Candlestick lamps with black shades are fairly easy to find. Look for them in better home catalogs and in fine furniture stores.

Accent this quietly elegant table with elements such as an English butler and brush, used to brush food crumbs from the tablecloth. Set glass oil-and-vinegar cruets in silver trays at opposite ends of the table and, if you wish, include such niceties as china butter chips, salt cellars, and knife holders.

Other Possibilities

- Instead of using a print tablecloth, substitute solid blue (the blue in the Blue Willow pattern) tablecloth. Use napkins printed with a blue-and-white Oriental design.

- Rather than folding the napkins, tuck them into silverplated napkin rings.

- Add a spark of warm color to the centerpiece by arranging a cluster of red, yellow, and pink roses in the vase.

- In place of the willow dinnerware, use any traditional designed pattern. Coordinate the tablecloth and the china.

- Practice a variety of napkin folds so you will have a wide repertoire of napkin folds to choose from. Folding table napkins is an easy way to change the look of the table without acquiring new tabletop pieces.

Table That Memory

Encourage fond memories of past family gatherings. Tableware and memorabilia inherited from the family deserve to be served up in new ways, once again valued and used as a part of family life.

If you are fortunate to have inherited your family's dining table set, you will already have a solid start in enjoying your family's dining memories. The well-worn patina your dining set exhibits can't be duplicated by a new set, no matter how expensive. Even Johnny's toothmark on the edge of the table can be treasured for what it is, a testament of personalized family use.

Handed-down table linens are a treasure, too. Old linens should be hand-washed in hot water, laundry soap, and a small amount of chlorine bleach. For silk items use a powdered nonchlorine bleach. For embroidered linens, iron on the wrong side with a fluffy towel underneath. Experts advise never to dry clean old cotton or cotton/linen combinations.

Tears in lace and crocheted pieces can sometimes be reworked or replaced. Fold your linens differently each time you put them away so that you don't weaken the fabric along the same fold line. Better yet, wrap the linens around a tube. If you don't use your antique linens often, store them in acid-free tissue paper.

Informal cotton tablecloths are becoming decorator items, too, especially the 1950-printed cloths. Unfortunately, many tablecloths have stains on them that can never be removed. If you can't hide a stain with a strategically placed plate or centerpiece, consider cutting the stain out of the tablecloth. Depending on where the stain is, you should then be able to fashion a smaller cloth, a runner, or placemats from the original piece. Think about making chair cushions out of remnants, too.

After all is said and done, there is nothing like family heirlooms from the homestead. When it's time to portion out the estate, let the other family members choose the grandfather clock, the rocking chair, and so forth. You busy yourself finding treasures for your table memories.

Glassware is always a welcome find. Usually by this time, pieces are missing from the set. Of the glassware that remains, there are likely to be a few chipped pieces. If the chip in the lip of a glass isn't too deep, you can take it to someone who has the equipment to sand and buff the chip smooth. Ask your antique dealer for names. Since matched sets of tableware are just a little ordinary, feel free to mix other glasses, new or old, to make up the number you need.

The same advice holds true for the dinnerware. Don't fret if you don't have a complete set. Mix and match the pieces in each place setting, or alternate place settings to reach the number you need.

Although picture frames aren't usually thought of as tabletop ware, they can contribute to your memory table. Tabletop picture frames with ornate trim are especially nice to frame a dinner menu. Small miniature frames fitted with the guest's picture make unique place cards. Or simply write the guest's name in beautiful penmanship and slip that in the miniature frame.

Brooches and medals from the family jewelry box can highlight the table. Use them as accents to swag a tablecloth. Catch the top points of each swag with a brooch or medal. Tie lengths of $1/8$-inch-wide, color-coordinated ribbon to the brooch or medal and finish in a bow. Let the ends of the ribbon fall freely.

Other Possibilities

❧ Use Grandmother's kitchen utensils, such as nutmeg graters, apple corers, or stovetop coffee pots as focal points for country-styled centerpieces.

❧ Use seldom-used pieces such as salt cellars in a new way. Put tiny flower petals or a blossom in them and set them at each placesetting as individual centerpieces.

❧ If a precious handed-down piece — a crocheted tablecloth, for instance — is beyond repair, commission a new piece to duplicate it. The design will call forth long-forgotten memories.

Seasonal Settings

New Year's Eve
Winter Tropics
Valentine Hearts
Easter Bonnet Buffet
A Breath of Spring
Mother's Day
4th of July Celebration
Summer-ize Your Table
Trick or Treat
Fall's Football Follies
Giving Thanks
Holiday Festivities

New Year's Eve

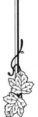

Ringing in the New Year is a time-honored tradition, a time when good friends gather at the dining table. This auspicious moment demands a beautiful and lavishly set table.

All is white and glittering on this late evening dinner table. Begin with a full white damask tablecloth laid end to end with at least a 10-inch drop on each side of the table. A dramatic floor-length cloth is an alternative.

Place matching white napkins, dinner sized, next to the plate at each place setting. Fashion a napkin ring from a 1-inch silver ribbon. Stitch the ends of a length of ribbon together to make a circle the size of a napkin ring. A small bow made from another piece of silver ribbon can be tacked over the joined ends of the ring. To give a finished look to the napkin ring, attach a tiny diamond-dusted pine cone to the bow. First collect or buy tiny pine cones. Cover them with a thin glaze of glue, and sprinkle silver glitter on them. Then glue a pine cone to the center to the bow.

The best kind of dinnerware to choose for this table is white with contrasting trim or a white pattern on a white background. For example, any white dishes bordered with a contrasting color with or without a band of silver or a white-on-white dish, like a Wedgewood pattern, will add to the white-and-silver look.

A large silver bowl filled with silver ball ornaments makes a stunning, light-catching centerpiece. Attach silver and white confetti-filled balloons to hover overhead. Add a tablespoon of confetti to the balloons before blowing them up. Tie three or four of the helium-filled balloons to silver balls and tuck those balls beneath the other balls in the bowl. Then attach air-filled balloons to the overhead light fixture and let them fall toward the centerpiece. At midnight, pop the balloons to add more noisemaking to the occasion and in the process drop a shower of confetti on the table and guests.

Set votive candles in glass containers around the bowl. Or stand short pillar candles on silver dishes, trays, or trivets. Set an uneven number of three or five candles at intervals around the silver bowl.

For celebration purposes, arrange a selection of snappers, horns, and paper hats above each place setting. Garnish liberally with curly ribbon and silver confetti. For good measure, sprinkle confetti and curly ribbon pieces over the entire tabletop.

If noisy gaity is your goal, set every alarm clock and radio in your home for the midnight hour. At the stroke of twelve, blow the horns, twirl the noisemakers, and pop the centerpiece balloons. Time the dinner so that dessert has been served and enjoyed just before midnight. Then sit back and enjoy the shower of confetti and well-wishing sounds of the New Year.

On the other hand, it is possible to celebrate the New Year in a more subdued manner. Again plan the dinner so the dessert course is served a little before midnight. Then a few seconds before the magic hour, pass a silver tray containing a selection of silver and white wrapped packages. Each guest will take and open one package, finding a New Year's resolution inside. Write these resolutions in either a positive or humorous mood. Other eye-catching ways to package the resolutions are in polished seashells, in silver-gilded walnut shells, or in small, attractively covered appointment books. Slip a resolution between the pages of each book. When the clock strikes twelve, everyone opens their package and toasts the New Year with champagne.

Other Possibilities

🍂 Toasting goblets are more festive looking with silver ribbon tied around their stems.

🍂 Set a few ceramic cherubs about the centerpiece and table to symbolize the infant year.

🍂 Chromium serving dishes can serve as a substitute for silver in this silver-and-white theme.

Winter Tropics

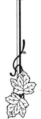

Warm up a winter evening with a tropical dining experience. A fantasylike, sensuous mood dominates this setting, letting you indulge your predilection for warm-weather tableware and accessories.

Many of the appointments for this table setting are found-again treasures from the closet or new findings at import shops. One such example is bamboo fans. You'll find most fans are just the right size for place mats. Their natural color and texture offer a tropical flavor, and they are easily cared for. Once dinner is over, simply wipe them off with a damp cloth.

These fans are particularly attractive when placed on a verdant green tablecloth. Otherwise, cover the table with a white, cream, or beige cloth and then lay large green leaves — ferns, for example — between the tablecloth and place mat. The greens should cover a larger area than the fan so the green leaves stick out around the place setting.

Build on this tropical place setting with clear summery glass dishes. Use a glass plate for the main dish and serve salad on green majolica dishes. Use a few majolica serving dishes to keep the salad plates company. Decorate the serving dishes with tropical blossoms like hibiscus or bougainvillea.

As for party favors, delight your guests with handpicked large conch shells, the kind one listens to for the sound of the ocean. Either share shells from a recent vacation or look for conch shells at an import shop. Present the shells in a small wicker tray or basket lined with plastic and filled with fine white beach sand.

Before dinner, serve tropical drinks in decorated coconut shells or palm-decorated poolside tumblers. Trim the glasses with pineapple wedges, cherries, and paper party favor umbrellas. During dinner, serve iced tea in hurricane-shaped glasses.

Hurricane glass shades over candles make a wonderful romantic addition to the tropical table. Set the candles in the center and spread a few greens around the base of the candles. Then arrange short branches of bougainvillea on top of the greens. Hibiscus blossoms dotting the green leaves are equally lovely.

If possible, serve the dinner on a wicker or bamboo-based table. For this one occasion, move the dinner to the four-season porch or move the patio bamboo furniture to the dining area. Carry the patio umbrella in with the rest of the furniture and open it wide over the table in the dining area.

Forest sounds are an integral part of the tropical scene. These, too, can be duplicated. During dinner, play tapes of bird calls and sounds of nature as background music. The sound of falling water, either taped or from a small room-sized waterfall, adds to the tropic moment.

And for a last bit of whimsy, place a ceramic or brass monkey on a side table or down on the floor as a doorstop. Just one more detail to complete the picture.

Other Possibilities

- Use colorful bamboo or reed place mats instead of fans for the place setting.

- Order a bouquet of flowers from the florist that includes tropical anthurium, orchids, or lacy fern.

- Inject a bright tropical note of color to the place setting by choosing napkins in hot pink. Tuck the napkins in napkin rings reflecting the same material used in the place mats.

- Set pots of bougainvillea and tropical green plants in odd corners and spaces of the area surrounding the dining table.

- Serve hot, spicy food to turn up everyone's thermostat.

Valentine Hearts

Cupid's arrow will hit its mark with this table setting. Pink, red, and white whimsical hearts popping up on the table and chairs emphasize this "heart-of-my heart" theme.

Cover the table with a white lace tablecloth underlaid with a pink tablecloth. The pink tablecloth will show through the lace tablecloth. A pink bed sheet can substitute as a tablecloth. Measure and cut the sheet to fit the lace tablecloth.

Set at each place setting one large glass dinner plate and one smaller glass plate. Insert a white paper heart between the plates. Craft hearts from white paper lace doilies. Cut out hearts a bit smaller than the small glass plate and glue a dried, pressed flower to the center. For extra detail, glue a tiny pink bow using $1/16$-inch ribbon to the stem of the flower.

Attention to detail will brighten the napkins, too. The napkins should match the pink tablecloth underneath the lace cloth. If you have used a sheet for the tablecloth, cut 20 x 20-inch squares from another pink sheet and machine-hem the edges. Take the center of the square napkin in your fingers, lift off the table, and shake loosely so that the edges of the napkin drape together. Tie a narrow length of white lace around the upper one third of the napkin, close to the pinched-together center.

Present a tiny heart-shaped menu to each guest. Cut 3-to-4-inch hearts from pink, red, and white construction paper. Punch a hole at the top center of each heart and tie the three hearts together with a $1/16$-inch ribbon. It can be the same ribbon used for the pressed flowers. Write or print one course of the dinner on each heart. If you have more than three courses, cut and tie more hearts. Place the heart menu directly above the glass plates. Fan the hearts out a little and lay on the table.

For the centerpiece, purchase a pink azalea plant. Gardenias or pink carnations are pretty in this setting, too. Cover the pot with bright pink foil and tie a length of white lace around the pot. Finish off with a loosely tied bow.

For a heart finale, tie a beautiful pink satin and white lace ribbon around the backs of the chairs. The ribbon should be at least 3-inches wide. Shape a large florist bow and add two more streamers so that there are four streamers falling softly down the chair. Add a lace-edged heart to the center of the bow. Make the heart by gluing lace around a construction paper heart. Glue the finished heart to the center loop in the bow.

Other Possibilities

🏵 Another tablecloth idea is to use a white tablecloth and glue pink and red foil hearts to the cloth. Use a glue that allows you to remove the hearts from the cloth without leaving a glue residue. This type of glue is available at craft stores.

🏵 An alternative to the traditional pink, red, and white color scheme is to use varying shades of purple, lavender, and white. Select lavender or white daisies.

🏵 Use wrapping paper as an underliner for the lace tablecloth. Purchase paper in rolls and roll out the correct length for the table. A pink enamel paper shines under white lace.

Easter Bonnet Buffet

Parade a cheerful mix of tableware, linens, and accessories on this buffet table. Because an exuberant look is the objective here, you can use a lighthearted approach to this traditional celebration.

An old-fashioned straw hat inspired by the song "Easter Parade" is the focus of this table setting. Adorn the table with a pair of his-and-her straw hats. A bon vivant's straw hat with a brim and encircled with a colorful fabric band is his. Her hat has a wide brim, flowers and bows, and a fabric scarf tied around the crown and ending in floating streamers.

Match the scarf and band around the hats to the buffet table-cloth. Use a dotted fabric in a springtime color or a bright solid color. Tuck one flower stem in his hat band, and arrange clusters of flowers on the brim of her hat. Intersperse ribbon bows between the blossom clusters.

Behind the hats set a tabletop tripod. Prop "Easter Parade" sheet music on the tripod. Search for the "Easter Parade" piece at antique and collectible shows. If you can't locate one, substitute handcrafted sheet music. Calligraphy the title on a sheet of paper and add a drawing of an old-fashioned Easter hat and musical notes.

In between the serving dishes set ceramic Easter bunnies and dyed Easter eggs. Write guest names in wax on some of the eggs before dying and make sure those eggs are prominently displayed on the table.

Set a bouquet of flowers on either side of the centerpiece. Set them so there is equal space between bouquet and centerpiece and between bouquet and the edge of the table. Select a crystal or glass vase or a container symbolic of the celebration, such as a rabbit, egg, or duck.

Arrange the serving dishes on the buffet in a way that makes it easy for guests to serve themselves. Set plates first and place the serving dishes close by. Then lay the flatware and napkins after the serving dishes for guests to hold under their plates. (For information about buffet napkin folds, see *Folding Table Napkins,* Brighton Publications, Inc.). The beverage service may be at the end of the table or close by at a smaller table.

The napkins should also be a dotted pattern in a soft cotton or rayon-and-polyester fabric. Match the colors of the napkins to the tablecloth or use contrasting colors. Either way, they'll lend a festive spirit and continue the lighthearted look.

Party favors may be offered at the buffet table, or at the beverage and dessert table, or at an individual table for the guest's seating. Choose a lovely assortment of tasty truffles and distribute them evenly into small grass-lined, straw-handled baskets. Tie a perky little bow on the handle of each basket.

If you choose to seat your guests at small tables, cover the tables with the same polka dot tablecloth. Instead of offering flatware and napkins at the buffet table, lay them out at each place setting. In keeping with the small size of the table, make a miniature centerpiece version of the table.

Other Possibilities

- Since bunnies are a must for Easter, prop a plush bunny next to a nest of dyed Easter eggs in unlikely spots, such as the entryway, a corner of a hallway, or the hearth of a cold fireplace.

- Play traditional spring music softly in the background. Some titles you could use are "Easter Parade," "Here Comes Peter Cotton Tail," and "Singing in the Rain."

- For a more sophisticated Easter centerpiece, arrange stems of Easter lilies in a clear round tall glass vase. Arrange a layer or two of dyed Easter eggs in the bottom of the vase.

A Breath of Spring

Soft, springlike colors, perky, fresh table linens, and party favors suggesting new growth whisper a promise of longer days. If spring is here, can summer be far behind?

Begin the setting with a fabric that has been a favorite for some time, a fabric that fairly sighs, "It's Spring!" . . . white pique. Pique is a firmly woven cotton fabric with the appearance of tiny ribbed or corded squares. It's a very fresh, textured look. Select place mats (or make your own) in this fabric, either edged in ruffles or with a self-binding finish.

Napkins should be of soft cotton. Either pick one solid-color pastel or choose a variety of colors like pale green, blue, butter yellow, peach, aqua, and pink.

The party favors emphasize spring's promise of summer. Fill tiny clay pots with a packaged potting soil then drive a white stake into each pot. Glue seed packets on the stakes. The packets should contain cool-weather plants such as pansies, sweet peas, lettuce and assorted greens, or herbs. Tie three ⅛-inch ribbons (each a different color) around the pots and finish with a multihued bow.

If you have extra time, spray-paint the pots in the same pastel colors as the napkins. Another alternative is to mix spackling compound (a powdery substance mixed with water to form a paste that dries hard, used to fill cracks and nail holes in walls). For texture, sprinkle a little lint from the clothes dryer into the mixture. Then mix a drop or two of paint, just enough to suggest a color, into the compound. Now it's ready to smooth on the pots. This method will give a wonderful stylish texture to the outside of the pots.

When there are more than six dinner guests, the party favors can be used as name cards, too. Simply write the name of each guest on the top of each seed packet with a black marking pen.

Dinnerware in this setting. should be light and informal. Either simple pottery or stoneware is appropriate. Pale colors or a pretty floral pattern will continue the light and fresh mood.

Popular French provincial dinnerware seems designed for this table setting. Neither elaborate nor plain, it's simply charming. The design is curvy, the pattern is usually tiny country flowers, and the colors can be bright or light. In this setting, light pale colors are best. Pitchers and tureens are often available as accessories.

For accent, goblets of lightly tinted glass make a nice addition to the pale colors and the light touch of the table design. Fill a pitcher full of spring daisies. They should be arranged loosely and informally.

Other Possibilities

🍂 Classic English floral tableware can provide a quite different mood to the spring table. The pattern inspired by field and garden flowers is light and fresh, but the overall mood is more formal.

🍂 The more formal spring table is a good time to show off a collection of delicate floral porcelain pieces such as name card holders, salt and pepper shakers, or napkin rings.

🍂 Spring bulbs make a lovely statement for the table setting, too. Arrange a bouquet of tulips or daffodils for the centerpiece, and present a single tulip bedecked with long, pale-colored ribbon streamers at each place setting.

🍂 The menu itself can declare the coming of spring. Asparagus as an appetizer, lamb as the main dish, and pistachio ice cream and a butter cookie for the dessert course freshen the winter palate.

🍂 Birds are an integral part of the spring scene. So, if you have just one or a collection of porcelain or ceramic birds, happily display them on the table.

Mother's Day

Set a stylish table that says "Happy Mother's Day" . . . and reminds her of your affection. Flowers and ribbons with lavender and lace create a memorable table. She'll be doubly appreciative.

Dress the table with a striped lavender-and-white tablecloth. A shiny fabric such as moire rayon or acetate with a watered or wavy pattern or a glossy satin fabric decides the style of this table setting. Use the fabric as a table skirt with a white lace top cloth, or reverse the look with a simple white tablecloth topped with a square of striped satin laid kitty-cornered.

Lavender-and-white floral napkins edged with lace continue the color scheme but insert a slightly different look because of the floral print. The tablecloth, and napkins do not have to be exactly matched. In fact, you can select a plaid lavender-and-white napkin or simply one color like a darker shade of lavender to make an interesting combination with the striped lavender tablecloth.

Sometimes one has to work with what is at hand. An alternative to the striped tablecloth can be a lavender cloth or a lavender-and-white floral print. Then simply reverse the selection of the napkins. Choose striped napkins or perhaps dotted lavender napkins.

This occasion calls for an arrangement of dendrobiums, the orchid lover's orchid, in the center of the table. Select three or more sprays and arrange in a crystal vase. Scent-filled dendrobiums display as many as fifteen blossoms on a graceful arching spray. The blooms vary from pale lavender to deep purple.

If not at each place setting then certainly at the guest of honor's place setting, a nod should be made to the time-honored custom of the Mother's Day orchid corsage. Instead of a corsage, nestle a pastel-hued orchid in a cloud of baby's breath shown off to perfection in a keepsake perfume bottle. In Victorian times, a fine perfume bottle became a treasured keepsake for the dressing table. Lay the stopper of the perfume bottle on the table close to the bottle.

To embellish the setting even more, tie a satin lavender ribbon around the mimosa goblets. Perhaps tuck a tiny dried white rosebud and baby's breath in the bow.

Other Possibilities

🦋 Change the centerpiece to suit your guests' tastes. Fill one large straw basket and tiny individual straw baskets with fragrant white freesias and white rosebuds. Line the basket with silk green leaves. Entwine the handles of the baskets with lavender ribbon and finish off with a pretty French memory ribbon.

🦋 If the guest of honor is a young mother, help the youngsters to handcraft a centerpiece and party favors. Buy small plants at the nursery and have the children pot them in lavender paper cups, enough for each place setting. Then have them choose a favorite plant of Mom's (three small plants or one large one) and tie lavender ribbon around the pots for the centerpiece.

🦋 Combine the centerpiece with a Mother's Day gift. Highlight Mom's interests — music, sports, literature, hobby — when arranging the centerpiece. Tuck into a bouquet of flowers a representative piece of sports equipment, a CD for her music enjoyment, or tickets to a special event of interest to her.

4th of July Celebration

*The 4th is a day for a flag-waving cele-
bration. It's time to razzle-dazzle your
guests with tables exploding in a display of
patriotic fervor.*

Color your table in patriotic red, white, and blue. A blue tablecloth presents a basic background on which to arrange red, white,
and blue dinnerware and accessories.

If this is to be a large gathering, group picnic tables outside on
the lawn and patio. You'll need inexpensive table coverings for
such a gathering of tables. Decorative paper tablecloths are always
an option, but they do tear easily and often flap about in the slight-
est of breezes.

Bed linen sales are a good solution. If you're using a portable
table 60 x 30 inches, purchase double sheets. By cutting these in
half crosswise, you will have two tablecloths 81 x 54 inches.
Allowing 1 inch for a single hem will give about a 10-inch overhang
on a 30-inch-wide table. For longer tables, seam across the 54-inch
selvage. For small tables, cut the sheeting to size.

A round patio table with umbrella can be included for extra
seating. Either use the tablecloth you normally would use for this
table or cut a round including an extra 10 inches for the overhang
out of the same sheets. For the sake of convenience, sew a heavy-
duty zipper from the edge to the center of the opening for the
umbrella pole.

Select a medium or dark solid-colored blue as a background to
build a patriotic mood. Since truly blue flowers are hard to find, it is
easier to build on the blue color with the cloth, tableware, or accessories.

Fabric napkins in a blue-and-white or red-and-white stripe or
paper napkins in a patriotic pattern such as an eagle blend into the
overall look. Tuck the flatware into the fabric, and especially the
paper napkins, to keep the napkins from blowing about.

Red and white flowers are plentiful at this time of year. Choose from gladiolus, carnations, and geraniums to name a few. Blue delphiniums are available at this time of year, too, so it is possible to arrange a patriotic-colored centerpiece.

Before putting the flowers in a container, anchor lightweight vases by dropping florist pebbles into the bottom. Another solution for a windy day is to arrange short-stemmed flowers in a low shallow container.

Lend a little sparkle to the table by inserting sparklers into the flower arrangement. Tuck the stems of the sparklers in the green foam used in the shallow containers. A small box of sparklers placed at the top of each place setting could be enjoyed by the guests as party favors. Tie red, blue, and white curly ribbon around the boxes.

In a dining room you have the room itself to frame the elements. Outdoors, — a much larger area — you'll have to make sure the decorative accessories are large and bright enough to make an impact. Red, white, and blue bunting or ribbons can be strung up between trees and buildings. An American flag should also be waving from a pole somewhere in the area. And finally, frame the American Declaration of Independence on a large white poster. To make it look old, sear the edges with a flame. Tack this up on a nearby tree to refresh everyone's memory and to remind your guests of the real reason for coming together to celebrate.

Other Possibilities

- If you are planning to use paper plates, be sure to buy the heavy-weight kind. Heavy, strong paper plates make handling easier, and they are less likely to blow about or tip in the wind.

- Plastic tableware for outside use is always a good choice by a small group. Insulated pitchers and mugs keep beverages hot and cold, and plate trays and serving pieces are easy to transport.

- Strings of red Mexican peppers forming swags across the table provide patriotic color but with a slightly different flavor.

- A bowl of luscious red strawberries or deep red cherries with an accompanying bowl of brown sugar and sour cream dip can provide centerpiece color as well as a great ending to the meal.

Summer-ize Your Table

Achieve a summery effect by doing away with heavy tablecloths and fussy appointments. Florals and sun-kissed colors reflect the special brightness of the summer months.

A casual but smart summer setting offers a floral print tablecloth displaying a mix of pink, orange, red, and yellow bright and hot colors. The dinnerware, informal and carefully chosen for its color and harmony with the tablecloth, continues the statement. For example, a gay peasant or Mexican pottery in a harmonizing color flanked by blue or green Mexican glassware adds beauty and a simple joyfulness to the tabletop.

Then add to this creation a centerpiece of garden snapdragons in mixed colors and intricate blossoms. Seasonal garden flowers in bright colors always contribute to the exuberance of a warm summer's day.

A reed basket or a glass bowl of fresh lemons, limes, and oranges is an equal exchange for a bouquet of garden flowers. Place any available green leaves so the leaves extend out from the edges of the bowl.

The luncheon or dinner table planned for hot weather might include, in addition to the water glass, an iced tea glass to the right resting on a small plate. The flatware is placed in the usual way — iced teaspoons on the table to the right. If the glasses were to be served on a tray, the spoons would then be on the saucers.

When setting a table for a dinner marking a special occasion, take a somewhat more formal direction but still apply a light touch. White china stands out dramatically on a blue organdy cloth appliquéd in a pretty white floral pattern. Extend the white color of the appliqué to the napkins. Choose white cotton or cotton-and-polyester napkins. Lay the napkins, simply folded, to the left of the place setting.

Sparkling crystal glassware and the silver glint of flatware lend beauty and richness to this formal table setting. Continue the glitter with silver serving dishes and a crystal bowl of cut flowers. Select white flowers, such as lilies, phlox, or anything similar and arrange in a loose fashion.

Set silver candlesticks with tall white tapers on either side of the flowers. The tapers should be above eye level to avoid getting in the guests' line of vision. Always keep the candle flame either above or below the seated guests' line of vision.

Less formal but still elegant, this table setting suggests coolness and lightness, something to be savored on a hot summer's night. Set open lace-worked place mats with matching napkins on the surface of a beautiful polished wood or glass table. Select delicate floral china to complement the delicate beauty of the place mats. Cool the look of the table setting further with the addition of pale frosted glassware. This look can be repeated with a collection of pale frosted candles, some short, some tall, centered on the table. Use available greens underneath the candles. The greenery will provide contrast to the lace runner that matches the place mats.

Set tiny individual flower vases at each place setting featuring a rosebud or day lily. Another idea is to simply lay a silk flower above each place setting

Regardless of style, these tables exemplify summertime dining. Each setting is a complement to the carefree spirit of the season.

Other Possibilities

🌿 Use clear glass dinnerware over a bright summerlike print or solid-color place mats.

🌿 When planning a dinner in summer, consider moving the dining location from the formal dining room to the seasonal porch or patio area.

🌿 To tempt appetites depressed by hot weather, present a light menu in a pleasant environment.

Trick or Treat

Add some tricks to the table when it's time to treat your guests. With a few additions and alterations to the everyday table setting, you'll satisfy the most spook-addicted guest.

Since there will be many Halloween symbols and colors added to the table, simply lay a white or cream-colored tablecloth on the table. Then set the table with your everyday dinnerware and flatware. You can build a suitably weird party table from this basic foundation.

Start by decorating the beverage glasses. Purchase plastic water glasses or wine goblets from a party supply store. Then with black and orange markers, draw a smiling pumpkin or any other Halloween motif your artist's instincts desire.

In the center of the table, place a scooped-out pumpkin. Draw a fierce or smiling face on both sides and fill it with water. Arrange chrysanthemums, garden coxcomb, and glycerine-treated autumn leaves in the pumpkin. Tuck some glycerine autumn leaves under and around the pumpkin. You can use natural leaves picked up in your yard, but they will crumble quickly and aren't as easy to work with.

At this time of year, you should be able to find small candles in the shape of goblins, cats, witches, and pumpkins. Set these at random on the table. You can depend on small plastic pumpkins to produce a cheery glow when a lighted candle is placed inside.

To create the proper spooky atmosphere, exchange yellow bulbs for the white bulbs in all the dining area fixtures. Dim the lights if possible. Twine strings of electric pumpkin lights on the ceiling and above the table.

While you still have the step stool out, hang paper cutouts of spiders, goblins, witches, and cats with humped backs from the ceiling. Fix the cutouts to the ceiling with tape and monofilament fishing line. Hang them at different heights from the table.

Use paper cutouts to decorate the backs of the chairs. Tape a different Halloween figure to the back of each chair. Party stores and card shops have paper skeletons, ghosts, bats, and so forth that are a good size for the chairs.

Lay fabric or paper orange napkins to the left of the plate underneath the forks. Then place a personally decorated eye mask that is meaningful to each guest next to the place setting. It could be a favorite color, hint at a guest's occupation (such as dollar signs on the rim for banking), or serve as a reminder of a favorite literary character. This party favor may come in handy in case your guests want to indulge in a little trick-or-treating themselves.

Other Possibilities

🍂 In place of or on top of the tablecloth, run strips of black plastic sheeting, sold in garden supply stores. Draw place setting outlines on the plastic with neon markers.

🍂 For a festive look as well as easy cleanup, use Halloween-designed paper plates and cups.

🍂 Play weird or scary theme music to add more atmosphere to the setting.

Fall's Football Follies

With fall comes the football season. Let the luncheon table before the game or the dinner table that follows it take on the enthusiasm and high spirits of the main event.

Since this is a fairly informal occasion, textured linens and earth-toned pottery can be used to set the table. A nubby-textured gold- or beige-textured gold or beige tablecloth with matching napkins will harmonize with most teams' colors. On the other hand, instead of matching napkins, choose napkins that represent the favorite team's colors. Either fabric or paper napkins are appropriate in this setting.

The same informality applies to the choice of glassware and flatware. Heavy pressed thumbprint glass goblets or plain tumblers, either clear glass or tinted, will harmonize with the earth tone pottery. Plastic or ceramic mugs decorated with the home team's motif is another possibility.

The colors of the team you are rooting for influence the basic color choice of the centerpiece and accessories. Ask your local florist to fill one of your own containers with flowers closely matching the team's colors. Mums or daisies can be dyed to match. If you can find a ceramic vase in the form of a football, use that as the container for the centerpiece flowers.

If dinner is the main event, use candles on the table. Find candlestick holders or at least candles that will represent the team's colors.

Another easily arranged centerpiece can be made by banking bright red fall leaves on a wooden tray and setting a representative object of the home team, like a plastic helmet, in the center. Use craft-store oak leaves that are preserved with glycerine. The glycerine prevents the leaves from drying and becoming crisp and hard to handle.

Since there is usually some betting going on at these home

events, make it part of the tabletop decor. On this occasion, placing the winning bet is more luck than skill. That's because the winning numbers are placed underneath the plates at each place setting before the game. The guests won't know what number will be at their place setting. Write numbers from 0 to 9 on slips of paper or circles cut out of construction paper. Use a color that is representative of the home team.

Here is how it works: At the end of the first quarter, if the score is 7 to 6, you add the scores together and take the last digit — in this case, 3. Award prizes at the end of each quarter. When there are more than ten people, do the first 0 to 9 numbers and then start over at 0 until you have enough numbers for everyone. If one of the doubled-up numbers wins, then the two winners split the money or are awarded a prize each. If there are less then ten people, for example eight guests, then two place settings will have two numbers.

Prize money comes from an agreed-upon money pool. For example, if there are ten people and everyone puts $5 in the pool, then the first-quarter winner wins 10 percent, or $5 of the pool. The second-quarter winner wins 20 percent, or $10 of the pool. The third-quarter winner wins 30 percent, or $15 of the pool, and the winner at the end of the game wins 40 percent, or $20 of the pool.

Prizes can be given in place of the pool money. Have enough prizes ready to give if the winning number is declared by two people. Give prizes that can be used at the next tailgating party. Assorted plastic tableware, cooler, hibachi, coffee mugs, and cold-beverage holders are possibilities.

Other Possibilities

- Arrange a bouquet of dried grains in two glass containers, the kind used to store pasta. Tie wide grosgrain ribbon matched in color to the team's colors around the necks of both containers.

- Serve up a casserole dish of miniature plastic footballs, motif-decorated key chains, sporting whistles, tiny pennants, and other miscellaneous team artifacts. Display it as a centerpiece, then use the miniatures as party favors for the fans.

Giving Thanks

This family festival table symbolizes the tradition of giving thanks at harvest time. A scene of warmth and bounty swirls around the focal point in this setting . . . the turkey.

An old-fashioned Thanksgiving table scene evokes memories of earlier American days. Then, as now, the harvest celebration was marked by a bounty of food on the table.

Because this is truly an American holiday, dinnerware in the early American style is well suited. Dinnerware motifs of fishing, hunting, gardening, and shipping fit nicely in the Thanksgiving table ambience. Early American dinnerware is heavy and soft edged. Its shape is round and hexagonal, often with a thin line of color bordering the edges.

Then there are favorite dinnerware sets, not expressily made to celebrate Thanksgiving, but often used for this occasion. One such pattern is "Friendly Village," depicting scenes from a New England village. These can be collected slowly through the years to ultimately end up as a treasured heirloom. A collector's set definitely adds to the family's Thanksgiving ritual.

For those of you celebrating Thanksgiving with a limited selection of dinnerware, depend on the table covering and other tabletop pieces to convey the warmth of the season. For example, use a quilted fabric to offer an early American feel and to blend with the colors in the dinnerware set. A quilt, crafted in the wedding ring or log cabin pattern, would be more than adequate to set the Thanksgiving scene.

A tablecloth of lace, damask, or a blend of cotton and polyester in white or color is a good foil for the special holiday dinnerware. Select a color scheme of neutrals and earth tones accented with red, green, orange, or yellow. Make napkins from quaint prints, gingham, or rough weave fabrics. Finish the napkins by cutting the edges with pinking shears, or fringe the ends by pulling threads.

Pewter, silver, copper, brass, tinted glass, wood, and wicker are good choices for the table's serving pieces and accessories. These materials can be found in napkin rings, goblets, pitchers, serving bowls, and salt and pepper shakers. A collection of pewter mugs, for example, strikes just the right note for this table setting.

Plastic-handled flatware is an ecologically accepted substitute for the bone or ivory that was so often used with early American dinnerware. Otherwise, any set of sterling, silverplate, or stainless steel flatware will do nicely.

The centerpiece can be ordered from the florist, and often all kinds of ducks carrying a bouquet of dried flowers, grains, and cattails on their backs can be found. Or make your own centerpiece. Find two horns of plenty: ceramic, wicker, or papier maché. Fill the horns of plenty with polished fresh fruit and vegetables and accent them with dried grains. Set each horn facing opposite sides of the table. For the children's table, a simple-to-do fanciful carved pumpkin will delight.

To emphasize the bounty of the season, liberally dot the table with filled preserve jars of fruit, pickles, and jams. Make fancy tops for the canning jars. Cut a round circle of gingham a little larger than the top of the preserve jar. Set the gingham circle on the top of the lid and screw the preserve jar's ring down tight over the fabric.

Other Possibilities

🐿 If Thanksgiving dinner is served in the evening, candles can be a warm addition. Pour tinted candle wax in inexpensive thumbprint-styled goblets. Place several on the table as accents.

🐿 Add more texture and color to the table with randomly scattered miniature pumpkins and warty gourds.

🐿 Make a swag of red and yellow fall leaves (use glycerine leaves from the craft store), and add clusters of polished or varnished nuts and bittersweet at intervals.

🐿 Invite an unexpected guest: Set a ceramic or plush squirrel in a nest of dried leaves.

Holiday Festivities

Tis the season for pine bough and ribbon bow, for silver bell and mistletoe. So shine the silver, spread the white damask cloth, and let the festivities begin!

Transforming your table for the holidays depends on a style and color plan. But first, stop and take into account the dining area decor before committing yourself to a tabletop theme. Pay extra attention to interior color.

Although some interiors provide the perfect background to the traditional red and green colors, others do not. For the dining areas that do not, there are alternative color choices for the table that still retain the holiday spirit. Try a color scheme of off-white, peach, and green. Or consider a silver and blue setting. Substitute a color of your choice for the blue. If all else fails, keep it simple with a green-and-white tabletop color combination.

If you only want to consider the red-and-green color theme, try these variations. Pack purple statice and red carnations tightly together in an 8-inch bubble bowl. Pair a bowl of bright yellow lemons and a vase of vibrant red roses. Nestle polished red apples in an evergreen bough.

If you use fresh greens on the table, be sure the stems have a water source. Either a moist floral foam or a vase of water will do. Dry greenery creates a fire hazard.

Arrangements of fresh greens and flowers is a possibility, but the gases emitted by the greens kills carnations and affects any other fresh flower. Greens and fresh holly are a better combination. Trim the holly stems occasionally and keep filling the vase with fresh water. You'll be rewarded with an arrangement that will last through the holiday season.

Pixie poinsettias, which come in 4-inch pots, make an interesting grouping and are compatible to most interior settings. Pixies, fuller than a single-head poinsettia, have several blossoms and more foliage. They can be found in standard poinsettia colors: red, white, and pink. Arrange a grouping of three pots in either an oval or round basket, but make sure there is a liner on the bottom so they can be watered. Cover the top of the soil and the space between the pots with Spanish moss. Then accent the plants with tinsel, pine cones, ribbon, or bells. Any trim used should relate to the dining area decorations.

Many other holiday centerpiece ideas are easy to match to the dining area's decor. Pile Christmas tree balls in an oversized clear glass brandy snifter. Select only those colors that blend with the colors in the room. Decorate a gingerbread house in colors copied from the dining area. Set prancing reindeer on the table and hang a garland of flower blossoms around their necks.

An ivy hoop is another centerpiece that is easy to make and easy to coordinate with the dining area theme. The ivy, usually English ivy or needlepoint ivy planted in 4-inch pots, is trained around a circular wire. You can personalize the ivy hoop with the same color and style elements you have used to decorate the rest of your room. Trail ribbons through the hoop and finish off with loops or a big bow on one side. If the hoop will be seen on both sides, trail the ribbon on both sides of the hoop. Add small pine cones at intervals around the hoop. Tuck the ribbon ends through bells and tie a knot to secure the ribbon. Greenhouses sometimes train ivy into tree shapes as well.

China or earthenware offer the most basic decorative element to the table. There are several traditional holiday motifs to choose from, ranging from a red-and-green Christmas tree to a Norwegian hearts-and-pines border. A very formal china with a holly motif can fit more easily into the contemporary decor. China with a gold or silver band fits into any holiday decor.

Other Possibilities

🌿 Other decorative centerpiece accessories that can be easily color-matched to the room's decor are tiny wrapped packages and artificial fruits.

🌿 Old-fashioned children's toys always add warmth to the Christmas table. Miniature sleds, a tiny rocking horse, wooden blocks spelling the word Christmas, and tiny plush animals sporting Christmas bows are delightful.

Menu Inspired

Best of Barbecue
Pizza or Pasta
Asian Table
Mexican Fiesta
Dessert Fanfare
Cocktails & Appetizers

Best of Barbecue

A down-home barbecue, hot and spicy, deserves a matching outdoor table setting. Flavor a casual selection of dinnerware with the addition of a few eye-catching but functional pieces.

First off, improvise a picnic table by balancing a 4-x-8 sheet of plywood on metal or wood sawhorses. Make sure the plywood is thick enough so it doesn't bow in the middle. Group benches or folding chairs around the table. Folding chairs are preferred because they offer back support.

Since the top of the table is rough plywood, you'll definitely need a covering. Choose a white or tomato red tablecloth. You'll discover the barbecue stains won't show as much on a red tablecloth. Select white-and-red striped napkins, and make sure they are large — at least 20 inches square — because of the job ahead of them.

Pair the napkins and flatware together to form a decorative unit. Roll the flatware in the napkin and tie tightly with a red grosgrain ribbon. Then stand the rolls upright in a white flower pot. If more utensils and napkins are needed, use two flower pots, one at each end of the table. Find whimsical paper or silk bumblebees or butterflies on stems to attach to each napkin roll. Craft supply stores are likely to have these. Set the pots in accessible spots on the table.

Field flowers or garden cuttings are natural centerpieces for this setting. Place two old white ironstone pitchers some distance apart on the table. These kinds of pitchers can be found at most antique shops. It's not necessary to find a matched pair because it doesn't matter if they are different in size or shape. Fill one pitcher with field flowers, perhaps Queen Ann's lace or black-eyed Susans. Then arrange a bouquet of garden flowers like snapdragons or bachelor buttons in the second pitcher.

Barbecues necessitate quenching beverages. Supply large,

heavy mugs for foaming cold beer and tall glasses for iced tea or ice water spiked with a lemon slice. Keep pitchers filled with iced water available on the table.

For eye appeal, feature ripe red tomatoes. Offer handfuls of cherry tomatoes for before-barbecue snacks. Collect two or three tomato juice cans. Clean out the insides of empty tomato juice cans, but keep the paper label on the outside of the can intact. Look for cans that have the brightest red tomatoes on the label. Fill with cherry tomatoes and set the cans on the table before the barbecue.

Use tomatoes to deliver a message, too. At each place setting set a large tomato with a toothpick-held banner proclaiming the occasion . . . Father's Day, Labor Day, or any day you would like to celebrate. Instead of proclaiming the holiday, use the banners as name cards for the table. Set the tomatoes on small saucers or plates before putting them on the table.

More tomatoes make a better menu. Stick crudites (carrot and celery sticks) into slightly hollowed out tomatoes, one for each place setting. Set the tomato on a green lettuce leaf on a salad plate. Set the salad plate to the left of the forks.

A barbecue menu usually includes foods difficult to eat gracefully. Did you know that picking up any barbecued food and eating it with your fingers is correct if it is done at a barbecue? Corn on the cob can be buttered and salted all at once or just enough for two or three bites. Breaking the cob in half make things a little easier. It is a big help if plenty of corn holders and butter brushes are made available. Eat watermelon with a spoon or fork and remove seeds from your mouth the same way they came in . . . with the spoon or fork. This information and other etiquette solutions to eating difficult foods can be found in Betty Craig's *Don't Slurp Your Soup: A Basic Guide to Business Etiquette* (Brighton Publications, Inc.).

Other Possibilities

🐝 Find an old 1950s-style kitchen tablecloth to use on the picnic table. Vegetables, flowers, or vines are often featured making an appropriate background for the barbecue theme of wild-flowers and fresh tomatoes.

🐝 Provide the barbecue chef with a tall white chef's hat along with tongs and apron. Make it a professional barbecue!

Pizza or Pasta

Positively inspired by a pizza or pasta menu, this table setting illustrates today's casual entertaining style. Flair and flexibility rather than expensive appointments make the tabletop inviting.

Substitute large, dinner-sized fabric napkins for the place mats that you would ordinarily use. The napkins should be at least 20 inches square. For this occasion, red-and-green solid-color or checked napkins will emphasize the menu's Italian influence. A half-and-half combination of polyester and cotton gives just the right texture.

Each place setting sports one large napkin draped catty cornered slightly over the edge of the table. The opposite napkin corner above the place setting is tied in a simple self knot. The knot should be tied at the very end of the corner. Tying this knot will drape the napkin in soft folds but still leave room for the plate and other place setting appointments.

In the center of the table, arrange another napkin from the napkin set as a diamond rather than a square. Take a handful of uncooked spaghetti, linguine, or angel hair pasta lengths and tie together in a bunch. Use ⅛-inch ribbons in the colors you've chosen for the place mats. Tie the ribbons tightly about one-third of the length from the top. Gently fan the pasta out, top and bottom. Set the pasta in a glass carafe or a clear glass vase.

If the napkins you are using for place mats are checked, choose a solid-color napkin in a color from one of the checks. On the other hand, if the napkin place mat is a solid color, lay checked napkins in the appropriate colors on the place setting. Fold them simply, so the interest is held in the placemats. The napkins should be a generous size, too.

Next to the centerpiece on either side, set a tray of candles. The trays can be simple salad or luncheon plates. Set three votive candles or one squat pillar candle on each tray. Choose white or red and green candles to harmonize with the place mat colors. The height of the candles should not be greater than one-third of the height of the centerpiece. Once the candles are in place, scatter pieces of pasta around the candles on the tray. Use the pasta you often see in craft projects, such as shells, wheels, and spirals.

Each place setting should have a stemmed wine glass. Tie a short length of ribbon, color coordinated, around the stem in a loose knot. Use simple earthenware dishes and stainless steel or silverplate flatware in an informal style.

Offer individual servings of grated Parmesan cheese in unusual or collectible items, such as antique salt cellars or butter chips. Use small antique spoons for serving spoons. A larger serving of Parmesan cheese can be served in a stemmed, saucer-styled champagne glass. Set the glass on a small plate and place a serving spoon next to the glass on the plate. Other serving dishes should include baskets lined with a color-coordinated towel or napkin to hold chunks of garlic bread. Hot pans of pizza or lasagna can rest on portable wooden cutting boards. To serve wine, set glass carafes of wine between guests, one carafe for two guests. If you wish, tie a ribbon around the necks of the bottles.

Other Possibilities

❧ If red and green doesn't coordinate with your tableware and room decor, use any appropriate color. Just remember to coordinate place mats, napkins, and ribbon.

❧ Instead of the pasta centerpiece, substitute a cylindrical glass vase filled with alternate layers of cherry tomatoes and fresh brocolli florets in the center of the table.

❧ Because of the type of menu, provide extra napkins. Simply roll up extra napkins and set them upright in a tall narrow basket or lay them flat in a long shallow basket.

Asian Table

Entertain with an Asian motif combining visually appealing Asian ware with Western-style plates and bowls. As long as the overall patterns harmonize, the table will reflect grace and charm.

The most widely prepared Asian foods are still Japanese and Chinese. These two cultures have elevated the presentation of food to a fine art.

To the Japanese, the appearance of the food and the appropriateness of the dish are as important as the food itself. Its large influence in the recent food trend — nouvelle cuisine — with its small but attractive servings, typifies the attention to presentation.

The Japanese prefer to serve many foods in small quantities in an assortment of small bowls and dishes. Utensils and dishes are chosen to enhance the appearance of specific food. For example, a polished wooden plate makes an excellant sushi server. But you don't need to serve exotic Japanese foods to present a Japanese theme. A few pieces of brightly colored melon or two or three spears of asparagus on a black lacquer tray are very appealing.

Western plates and bowls are typically round, whereas Japanese dishes come in a variety of shapes, such as square or rectangular serving plates and octagonal bowls. It's a small matter to combine a few of these Japanese shapes with any plain Western stoneware or porcelain plates and bowls to strike a note of cool simplicity.

Ikat-patterned (tie-dyeing weft or warp yarns before weaving) place mats are definately the table covering of choice. However, simple casual, woven place mats in solid colors certainly are an adequate solution for the tabletop.

For the centerpiece, you may want to practice the art of ikebana, the Japanese art of arranging cut flowers in rhythmic decorative designs. Or arrange a small vase of pompom chrysanthemums at each place setting. Pompoms signify long life and happiness in many Asian cultures.

A typical Chinese table places less emphasis on the design of the dishes themselves but streses the serving of several courses. And unlike the Western menu in which the soup course is offered only once, soup is enjoyed often throughout the meal. Consequently, a number of bowls as well as plates are needed to see one's way through a typical Chinese meal.

The Chinese were the developers of porcelain and lent their name "China" to dinnerware. This term is often used when talking about any kind of dinnerware. Many blue-and-white porcelain dishes were exported to the United States and now, like Canton china, have become pricey collector's items. But other blue-and-white china is still being made in China and can be found easily at budget prices.

Serving dishes such as soy sauce carafes are available at certain tabletop shops and import shops. Craft shows are often good sources of teapots and teacups. Chopsticks, from green bamboo to nonslip red, can be purchased and set next to the utensils on chopstick rests. Chopstick rests are widely available, too, and are sold in sets.

Other Possibilities

🌿 Pass scented rolled towels at the end of the meal. Scent terrycloth fingertip towels with a favorite light cologne.

🌿 Set flowering branches of blooms in shallow pebble-lined containers as an alternative centerpiece.

🌿 Cut two lily blossoms off at the main stem. Put each blossom in a container such as a miniature pot or a glass tumbler. Tuck one green leaf in the pot underneath the lily. Group pebbles around the two containers.

🌿 Asian table manners include the use of toothpicks at the dinner table. Offer toothpicks in an attractive toothpick holder.

Mexican Fiesta

When your menu is Mexican minded, a south-of-the-border theme is indicated. Import colorful and lighthearted tableware and accessories to richly display the festive feast.

Lay fabric pieces in strong vibrant colors across the table. Serapes, rugs, or striped table runners in multi-hued colors are all good choices to serve as a fitting background to a spicy-hot, fiesta-fare menu.

Supply striped napkins to match the table covering or solid-color napkins, each one a different color, but all colors inspired by the table covering. Open the napkins to a full square, make a triangle, and then tie the triangle in a loose knot. Lay the napkin to the left of the place setting.

Another napkin possibility is to pull the napkins loosely through a pierced, tin napkin ring. The vibrant colors of the napkin will show through the pattern in the napkin ring.

The centerpiece goes green with a combination of green bananas, green limes, and a pineapple. Loosely arrange the fruit on a Mexican tin tray or flat pottery dish. Red peppers give a touch of contrasting color, as do lemons. Red chilies really add a sizzling accent.

Tin soup cans can be spur-of-the-moment candleholders. Empty or find empty soup cans, clean the inside, and remove the paper from the outside. Scrape off any glue residue. Then take an ice pick or use a sharp nail and hammer and punch a pattern around the can. Do a simple repeat geometric design or design a sunflower burst on each side of the can. Set a small votive candle inside each can.

Set several of these tin candleholders on the table so they form a ribbon of light down the length of the table. Mexican sashes, found at import shops, add more color when they are wound in and about the candleholders and centerpiece. Another way to use the sashes is to tie one on the back of each chair. Tie it loosely and let the ends fall where they may to give a touch of festivity to the chairs.

Paper cut-out banners commonly found in Mexican import shops strung around the edge of the table fashion a short table skirt. These paper banners come in a variety of colors, and each paper piece is about the size of a place mat. Six or eight of these pieces are strung together. These cut-out banners are very eye-catching when hung at ceiling height. They are also very effective hung from ceiling beams or stretched from tree to tree if the party is out-of-doors.

A variety of serving pieces made expressly for Mexican menus are available now. Terra cotta taco holders keep tacos standing upright, preventing lettuce and garnish from falling out. Sangria glasses as well as Mexican tinted glassware add another ethnic touch to the table. Fabric squares in strong, vibrant colors can be used to line taco and cornbread baskets.

A fiesta table benefits from a memorable party favor as well. Maracas, the small gourds with handles, are colorful and can add additional "music" to the party. Place one at the top of each place setting for your guests' enjoyment.

Other Possibilities

🐝 Arrange a centerpiece of Garbera daisies or zinnias in a glass jar; set in a straw basket.

🐝 Display miniature desert gardens of succulent plants and cacti in shallow terra cotta pots. Casually arrange two or three pots in the center of the table.

🐝 Use wrought iron trivets to keep hot serving dishes off the table.

🐝 Gaily painted Mexican tin Christmas tree ornaments are a good, inexpensive party favor idea. Tuck the decorations into the folded napkins.

Dessert Fanfare

A dessert-only occasion deserves a special presentation. Emphasize an international flavor with themed serving ware and table accessories. Visual reinforcement adds emphasis.

Serving a variety of desserts necessitates a buffet table. In the event this affair is for the benefit of a larger gathering like a fundraiser or a church activity, use card tables — one for each country.

A basic white tablecloth for the single buffet table allows you to drape separate areas of the table with a covering indigenous to the dessert country's origin. For example, a silk square from India, a shawl from Spain, or a sash from Peru makes a colorful statement.

Card table coverings can follow the same basic white tablecloth approach or use a tablecloth of Irish linen or Madeira lace to quietly understate the theme. Woven rugs can also be laid diagonally across the small table.

Demarcate each country's serving area on the buffet table with strips of bright ribbon representing the colors in the flag of that particular country. For example, red, white, blue for France; green, red, white for Italy. Check a dictionary or encyclopedia for other flag colors. On a small table, where only one country is represented, lay the ribbons in stripes across the table or kitty-cornered, diagonally.

If there are to be separate tables for each setting, tie groupings of helium-filled balloons to the table area. Select only the flag colors of that country and write the name of the country on one balloon in black felt-tip marker. Tie curly ribbon in the same colors around the necks of the balloons and let the ribbons fall freely down to the table. This gives height to the table setting and makes it easier for the guests to identify each table.

The centerpieces can identify the country, as well. If fresh or silk flowers are to be used, select them only in colors matching the flag colors. Or, choose a flower that is identified with a particular country: tulips for Holland, pompoms chrysanthemums for Asia.

Another approach is to use candles or ceramic pieces. For Italy, entwine a candelabrum with ivy and grapes or encircle a bust of Nero with an ivy garland. For Spain, prop an open fan on the table with a cluster of flowers at the base. For Russia, lay a circlet of flowers around the base of nesting dolls.

Dessert offerings can include gelato from Italy, choux à la creme for France, flan for Mexico, and last but not least, an assortment of ingredients for ice cream sundaes to represent the United States. Prop up cards of the dessert names written in that country's language and in English.

Offer the desserts on serving dishes that, if not authentic, are a reminder of that particular country. For example, use English Wedgewood, Japanese lacquer, Swedish lead crystal, Mexican tin, and Chinese blue-and-white porcelain.

Other Possibilities

🌸 Miniature flags of each country will add to the table decoration. You may find them at import stores. If you live in a large city, call the country's embassy for help.

🌸 Mound special candies made in or representative of each country in candy dishes and top the candy with a tiny flag.

🌸 Identify each area of the buffet table with a small item indigenous to the country. Write the country's name on a small fan from Spain or a half-bottle of Soave wine from Italy.

Cocktails & Appetizers

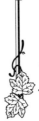

Cocktail party fare presents a challenge and an opportunity for imaginative table setting. This lively, informal presentation is flexible and varied.

Appetizers should be presented at a cocktail party in such a way that guests can stand and chat while enjoying a variety of bite-sized tastes. Miniaturized versions of favorite recipes should be offered on serving trays and platters.

As at any party, food should be prepared as much as possible beforehand. Serve one or two cold selections as guests arrive and then assemble the warm dishes. Some appetizers lend themselves to hands-on preparation by the guests. Whether it's grilling, broiling, or just spreading, guests preparing their own fare are part of the contemporary cocktail scene.

The party table itself should reflect the culinary selections. Since multiethnic influences have extended current eating styles, it's fairly simple to select an ethnic theme for the menu and the table. A judicious theme selection will increase the visual possibilities for your table.

You can borrow from the Thai culture and prepare delicious Thai-prepared kebabs highlighted with a flourish of tropical bamboo fans. To decorate the table, balance two fans on end behind the serving dishes. Then line a platter with an opened fan, and arrange the kebabs on top. Place a multihued Thai textile piece diagonally underneath the platter.

Food sampling from a Tex-Mex American mesquite grill will look and taste more authentic served on appropriate serving dishes. Select coarse pottery ware, the more oddly shaped and decorated the better. This is when all those vacation impulse pottery purchases will redeem themselves. Stick paper flowers in vases and serve sangria in green-hued, handblown glasses.

Toast the German Bavarian tidbits with beer served in glass

steins. Set the table with flower-laden crystal vases and line the serving trays with remnants of decorative lace curtains. Find a pretty cuckoo clock for the centerpiece.

Serve seafood cuisine underscored with a pirate theme. Find two large kegs to hold a rough-hewn plank for use as a table. Place bite-sized appetizers on silver serving platters and set between props of burlap bags filled with coffee beans. Drape burlap on the board as a kind of table runner. Contrast the texture of the burlap bags with silver pieces set askew. This is one time when slightly tarnished silver is appropriate. A silver candy dish is just right for the lemon slices for the seafood. Fill coconut half-shells and pineapple boats with seafood salad offerings to emphasize the pirate cove look. Sprinkle gold foil-wrapped coins about the table.

No matter the theme, every appetizer tray should be tastefully arranged and garnishments added. For seafood, offer lemon baskets filled with cocktail sauce. Use pimento strips, truffles, or radish slices to bring color to finger foods. Garnish serving plates with sprigs of fresh parsley or dill. Alternate green grape halves and red cocktail cherries for a holiday garnish.

It's a good idea to serve only drinks that can be made in quantity and can be poured from pitchers. This allows guests to help themselves, eliminating the need for a bartender. Besides pitchers, beverages can be served from punch bowls, blenders, bean pots, glass blocks, even fish bowls. Have a variety of glass sizes available. Good beverage garnishments to have at hand are lemon and lime slices, olives, maraschino cherries, lemon twist, and carrot and celery sticks.

Other Possibilities

- Use cocktail-size napkins. Have more than one per serving available because of the finger food menu.

- It's also a good idea to have plenty of coasters scattered about the room for people to use when they want to put their beverage glass down for a moment.

- If the guests are to help prepare the food, don't neglect to have the necessary tools at hand. Kebab spears, spreading knives, grill forks, and serving spoons should be readily available.

Celebrations

Preschool Birthday

Invite Mother Goose to this birthday table. Lighthearted tableware, place mats, and decorations, all treated in nursery rhyme manner, give each small guest a personalized place of enchantment.

Each place setting on this table is different, depending on which nursery rhyme character the child chooses. It's important, then, to find out beforehand every child's favorite nursery rhyme and favorite character. Besides dressing the birthday table, this information can be useful as a birthday party activity.

The main reason for collecting the small guest's nursery rhyme character is to help you script a short fantasy play incorporating the chosen character of each child. Make up simple lines. These can be one word or a phrase, depending on the age of the child. Collect bits and pieces of costumes and props so the children can have fun dressing up for their parts. Perhaps their parents can help with this.

After the play has been presented, have the children, still in costume, sit down at the table. Each child has a special place setting reserved for her. That is because you will decorate the place setting with her selected nursery rhyme theme.

To prepare this round table of nursery rhyme characters, purchase a piece of white paper, wide and long enough to fit your table (butcher paper can be purchased at craft or art stores). Trickle a light stream of white glue in random fashion on the paper. Before the glue dries, sprinkle glitter or sparkle confetti on the paper. Shake off the excess after the glue has dried. If you're worried about damage to your table, put a table pad or a thin blanket underneath the paper.

At each place setting, set a specially prepared paper place mat. Cut place mats from pale green, pink, blue, and yellow construction paper with pinking shears. With a darker colored crayon, draw or trace the outlines of several different poses of the child's favorite nursery rhyme character. Set a few crayons in a plastic cup at each place setting so that when it's time for refreshments, the child can fill in the outlines while waiting to be served.

Place cards are handy at this type of party to prevent any discordant conversation about who sits next to the birthday child. In this case, balloons tied to the chair can be used as a place card and a take-home party favor. Buy helium-filled balloons (have them filled on the day of the party) or tie air-filled balloons to a stick and fasten to the chairs. With a black marker, write the child's name on at least one balloon in the cluster.

Instant pictures of the children are something else that will bring easy recognition of who sits down where. As the children arrive and after each child is dressed in costume, take a snapshot. Place the picture at the individual's place setting. This, too, serves as a name card as well as a take-home party memory.

Let the birthday cake be the centerpiece. Decorate it with nursery rhyme characters, if you wish, to carry the theme through the table setting. If convenient, purchase a variety of solid-color plates, cups, and napkins so each place setting is set with a unique color.

Other Possibilities

- Drape crepe paper streamers from the light fixture over the table to the corners of the room. Tie balloons on the light fixture, too.

- Cut paper shapes of selected nursery rhyme characters and punch holes in the top and bottom. Thread a drinking straw through and stick the straw end in the beverage cup.

- Tear out sheets from paint-with-water coloring books for place mats, something the little ones can do while you're dishing up refreshments. It's nice, but not necessary, if the pictures are about nursery rhyme characters.

- If you want floating balloons above the table, use helium-filled balloons and weight the strings by tying them around small boxes of crayons or small toys.

Golden Birthday

The golden birthday date plays a festive and prominent role on this birthday table. Picture a setting displaying the special birthday date almost to the point of saturation.

The special golden birthday falls on the year that is the same as the birth date. For example, if the birth date is July 10, than the golden birthday is celebrated on the 10th birthday. Ten is the number that is prominently displayed on the table.

Accent a fresh flower centerpiece with fun and festive balloons. Use one party bag of fresh flowers and balloons standing upright, and another bag lying on its side on the table with flowers cascading out of the bag.

Stand a container of water inside the upright bag and arrange flowers. Tie gold helium-filled balloons to the handles. Cut out the birth date number from construction paper and paste to an airborne balloon. Use a glue stick and lightly apply glue to the back of the number, then stick the paper number to the balloon. If guests will be eating outside, be warned that balloons discolor and may shrink. Don't make the centerpieces too far ahead of time.

For the side arrangement, use a small 4-inch saucer and put water-soaked foam inside. Put the saucer and foam close to the opening of the bag and poke flowers into the side of the foam. Good flowers to use for this arrangement are alstroemeria and miniature carnations. Anything else will probably be too big. Use just one kind of flower or both, and fill in the arrangement with leather leaf or tree fern. Tree fern gives a lighter look.

To include the date of the birthday year whenever possible, find flower picks with the year to poke into the flower arrangement. Another way to include the birth date is to stamp the golden birthday number on the balloons. Rubber stamps can be found in gift shops, office supply stores, or party shops. Blow up the balloons and then stamp away. You can find ink pads in several different ink colors, so use the birthday celebrant's favorite color. Besides numbers, you may be able to find rubber stamps depicting cakes, candles, and clowns. Use your imagination to decorate the balloons.

Another way to display the date prominently is with appliqués on the tablecloth or place mats. Cut out the number appliqué in the color and fabric you desire. Apply a thin coat of pressure-sensitive liquid adhesive to the back of the appliqué. Let dry for 12 to 24 hours until completely dry. After that time, place the appliqué on the cloth. You'll be able to move the appliqué from place to place as many times as you like. If the appliqué loses tackiness after many applications, simply apply a new coat.

Create a total design on the tablecloth with these appliqués. Cut out numbers about 3 inches tall and place them askew on the tabletop and on the overhang. For a confetti look on the table, cut several different colors of the numbers.

The great thing about this adhesive is that you can lift off the appliqués and wash the tablecloth, and the cloth will be as good as new for the next occasion. This adhesive is wonderful for attaching holiday or celebration appliqués to the tablecloth or place mats. Use the same linens over and over for any occasion.

Other Possibilities

🍂 Decorate the birthday cake with a candle in the shape of the special number of the birthday rather than using the total number of small birthday candles.

🍂 You can use things besides fresh flowers as a centerpiece. For example, put a vest appliquéd with the birthday number on the celebrant's favorite teddy bear.

🍂 Provide your guests T-shirts with the golden birthday number silk-screened on the front. When everyone is seated around the table, there will be no doubt as to what birthday celebration this is.

Sixteen Candles

Sixteen is an age of casual style and constant activity. Coordinate the birthday setting to reflect this lighthearted spirit using fun accessories and fuss-free table appointments.

This age group always seems to be involved in 101 activities. For this reason, it may be wise to consider scheduling the birthday party as a before-school early morning breakfast or an after-sporting-event supper. In other words, an attempt to catch these kids on the run is better than no party at all.

The color theme can reflect the rainbow, displaying a smorgasbord of color. Or, conversely, choose one or two colors to represent the school's colors. Then again, if the birthday person is known to have a passion for a certain color, by all means color-key the setting to the preferred color.

Since most fifteen-year-olds are focused on getting their driver's license on the day they turn sixteen, there should be some decorative allusion to this fact of life. Here is one way to decoratively come to terms with a new driver in the house. Begin with sixteen balloons, all displaying the theme's colors and filled with helium. Anchor the balloons to a model car or a toy car purchased from the dime store. Use washers in the car if you need extra weight to hold the balloons down. Tie narrow streamers that say happy birthday around the necks of the balloons and let them fall down and about. To personalize the centerpiece, tuck into the car a conspicuous coupon for a one-time late-night use of the family car.

Little brothers or sisters can take part in the preparations by punching holes in various colors of construction paper and scattering the colored confetti on the tablecloth. Do the same with curly ribbon pieces 4 to 5 inches in length.

The family's everyday tableware is just fine for this occasion. The kids will enjoy the casualness. However, to give the table an extra kick, consider buying a few inexpensive fantasy dishes. Sets consisting of a serving bowl and individual bowls can be found in painted and shaped forms such as half of a watermelon or cantaloupe. These serving dishes can be used to serve and hold breakfast cereal or fruit in the morning or chili or soup for a late-night supper.

Fantasy-designed mugs can lighten the setting, too. Novelty mugs can be found sporting bird and animal head handles, such as pelicans, toucans, zebras, or elephants. Or purchase inexpensive jumbo-sized coffee mugs and use them for soup, hot chocolate, or individual servings of popcorn.

Dress up beverage glasses with gaily colored straws with fold-out paper replicas of fruit, such as apples, pineapples, or lemons. For the beverage itself, you can buy fruit-shaped ice cube forms filled with distilled water and ready to freeze. These ice cubes also come in fruit colors, gumball size.

Finally, display a party favor to the left of each place setting. Since most of the guests will have just passed their driver's test, or will within the year, a shiny new key ring will be appreciated. Personalize the key ring with the guest's name and the date of the party. Don't box the key ring, but rather tie a large bow around it and let the ribbon ends stream down into loose curls over the edge of the table. The key rings, personalized with the guests' names, will serve as place setting cards for the table.

Other Possibilities

🍂 If this is an all-girl sweet sixteen party, tie a satin ribbon around pink rosebuds and present as party favors. Gift the birthday girl with a dozen pink roses.

🍂 If the guest of honor is passionately involved in sports, dance, or drama, tuck two tickets to an upcoming event of interest into a bouquet of flowers.

Adult Birthday Party

Birthday tables are always special, no matter the age. The adult version may be a tad more sophisticated, but it should still nudge everyone into the proper festive spirit of things.

Puzzles are going to be the focus of the dinner conversation. In fact, puzzles are going to be worked on and completed through the dinner courses. You can make your own puzzles for this event. Before the dinner party, collect any photos you have of the guest-of-honor with each dinner guest. If you can't find enough pictures (there should be a puzzle for every two people) or enough pictures to feature every guest, you're going to have to sneak some impromptu photo sessions before the party. The point is to make sure every guest's picture is included in at least one of the puzzles.

Blow the photos up to at least 8 x 10-inch size. Paste or glue the photos onto stiff cardboard and then cut into puzzle pieces with a sharp knife. Sprinkle all the puzzle pieces in the center of the table as if they were large pieces of confetti.

As the guests are seated, explain that there will be two people on each team. The group as a whole must decide whether their partners will be on the right or the left. Then it's up to each team to decide what puzzle they are working on and to collect the pieces needed for their puzzle choice. The contest should be encouraged to continue through the dinner until all the puzzles are completed. The prize for being the first to complete a puzzle can be a devilishly difficult new puzzle. How rowdy the dinner party will become will depend on how competitive or how cooperative the teams are.

Now turn your attention to the rest of the table. Primarily, you'll be changing or adding features to the everyday table setting to make it birthday festive. But still, keep in mind that the puzzle projects will need a certain amount of table space.

A state-of-the-art birthday table demands, for one thing, wrapped gifts, but not for the guest-of-honor . . . for the guests!

Wrap party favors in colorful wrapping paper and elegant ribbon. Again, make the packages small so there will be plenty of room on the table for puzzles.

Select party favors keyed to the guest-of-honor's interest. Tennis anyone? How about giving sweatbands or a tiny racquet key chain? Music's the passion? Try tapes. Gardening? One miniature garden shovel or a packet of seeds for each guest should delight.

At the same time you're collecting the party favors, scout for comparable objects to be put into a container and used as a centerpiece. Garden items — toss into a wire vegetable basket or a cardboard seedling flat. Add vegetable greens to the assemblage. Golf accessories simply pile into an upturned golf hat from a favorite clubhouse. The idea is to pair items and container to the guest-of-honor's interest. After dinner, present the centerpiece as a birthday gift.

Now the only-last minute instruction is to serve the guest-of-honor's favorite food. And for heavens sake, keep the lights high so everyone can be sure to see the puzzle pieces!

Other Possibilities

🌿 The 40th-year birthday celebration deserves that special attention be paid to the person's age. Party supply stores have a variety of decorations honoring the 40th, but since the guest-of-honor is old enough to be entering a second childhood consider a remote-control car as a kind of birthday-cake-serving conveyance. This will be possible only if the car is large and flat enough to hold a dessert plate. Set the car on the table and hand the control to the guest-of-honor.

🌿 Whatever year is being celebrated, balloons are always an integral part of the festivities. Tiny balloons tied onto handheld sticks clustered as a bouquet in a vase, balloons hanging from the ceiling forming a canopy over the table, or helium floating balloons at each place setting add a never-fail party spirit to the table.

The Fiftieth Birthday

Welcome to the fabulous fifties! To set this table in proper fifties rock-and-roll spirit, you'll need to dig out all your memorabilia from the olden days.

A buffet-style table is easiest when the guest list is larger than ten or twelve people. Set up as a focal point, it easily becomes the decorating highlight of the event. You can place it against the wall or center it in an area that is convenient to serve the birthday fare.

Dress the table in white and pink: a white tablecloth and a pink gathered net skirt. Measure the netting 2½ times the length around the table to make sure you get a fluffy expanse of gathers. Take more pink netting and scrunch pieces into loosely formed balls and place between the serving dishes. Or tie lengths of netting into big bows and dot the table with those. You could also tack bows on the skirt netting.

Felt poodles, the kind used to decorate fifties circle skirts, could be cut out and tacked or pasted to the net skirt. Before putting the skirt around the table, dribble glue in spiral tracks up and down the skirt. Then sprinkle sequins on the glue before the glue dries. Shake off the excess.

Once the table is covered, style a centerpiece in the form of a pyramid. At the base of the pyramid, lay a collection of memorabilia from the fifties. Rhinestone-decorated sunglasses, packages of bubble gum, and Mickey Mouse hats will summon memories of those rock-and-roll days. Next arrange a bouquet of pink carnations softened with sprays of baby's breath in a medium-height glass vase. Then at the apex of the pyramid, center helium-filled balloons flying high with various Happy Fiftieth birthday messages. Anchor the balloons on sticks stuck in the floral bouquet vase.

Suspend an old collection of rock-and-roll 45-rpm records above the table. Fill in the collection by buying more records from secondhand shops, or borrow records from friends. In any event, have enough records so a veritable shower of oldies but goodies is hanging above the table.

Serving dishes should be selected befitting a menu featuring White Castle hamburgers, greasy french fries, and cherry colas. Pile the hamburgers on large heavy-duty serving plates. The higher the stack of hamburgers, the more impressive the table. Serve the cherry colas and any other beverage offering in replicas of the original soda trademark glasses.

Paper napkins are appropriate for this birthday table. Select pink napkins and have them printed with the guest-of-honor's name and the 50th birthday date. Printers that carry wedding reception supplies will be able to supply these personalized printed napkins. To complete the selection of tableware, any white china or pink-and-white paper plates and cups will continue the festive informality of the table.

Background music will add to "aren't the fifties grand!" spirit. Introduce into the evening's musical selections such songs as "Rock Around the Clock" and "A White Sport Coat and a Pink Carnation." Every once in a while, throw in a happy birthday song, either from the fifties or from more recent years.

Add more fifties flavor to the party by offering an assortment of theme-related party favors. In a tray (a fifties copy featuring that period's favorite bottled drink), spread such items as pointy-frame sunglasses, ponytail hair clips, and party hats and noisemakers. Depending on your largess, you could provide every guest with a white T-shirt bearing a painted symbol slogan of the fifties. Use fabric paints or crayons to decorate the shirts. Then give a T-shirt to each guest at the beginning of the party. The T-shirts, along with the decorated table setting, will signal a fabulous fifties occasion.

Other Possibilities

- Old fifties album covers lend a nostalgic touch to the table. Favorite oldies of the guest-of-honor can be featured.

- String a canopy of pink-and-white crepe paper over the table setting. Pinch the edges of the crepe paper streamers to make them curly. Twist the streamers gently as you tack them in place.

High School Graduation

Other than landmark birth dates, no other event is so eagerly anticipated as high school graduation. Present a table fresh and youthfully exuberant, with a promise of wonderful days ahead.

Buffet-style serving will give you the flexibility you'll need if this is an open house event. Set up one serving table and several smaller tables for guest seating. The smaller tables can be card tables, game tables, picnic or patio tables, or makeshift plank and bench tables.

Select a theme for the day and carry it out on a grand scale on the serving table and on a smaller version on each of the small tables. Since most graduates would like to think there is nothing ahead for the next three months but clear skies, blue water, and warm sand, select beach paraphernalia to decorate the tables.

For example, use colorful large beach towels to cover the tables. Depending on the sizes and shapes of the tables, overlap the towels. Rather than simply laying them side by side, spread them diagonally or criss cross them over the table in a casual manner. The towels need not be identical. As long as they are all bright colors, the total picture will be coordinated.

The serving table, which is the center of this party, deserves special attention. Set a straw beach bag at a focal point of the table — traditionally the center. Placing the beach bag at the corner of the table that is next to a wall can be an effective setting, too. Drape a flashy beach towel over one side of the beach bag and let the end rest on the table. Hang a pair of sunglasses over the edge of the bag by one of its bows. On the side of the bag that faces the guests, use different colors to cut out and paste letters of the guest-of-honor's name. Lean a beach hat or visor against the basket on the table. Set suntan lotion, a music tape or two, and seashells around and about the basket.

Then set the tableware, buffet style, on the table. Select brightly colored plastic plates, cups, and flatware. Stand the flatware in plastic tumblers, handles up, for easy reach, with forks in one tumbler, knives in another, and so forth. Offer terrycloth fingertip towels as napkins, or go more casual with paper napkins. Colors should be beach-towel bright.

On the smaller tables, where room is at a premium, set a small beach ball or a pair of plastic water rings in the center. Then on the beach cloth around the ball, scatter seashells, plastic nose plugs, and anything else you have on hand that is small and part of the beach scene.

At the beginning of the buffet setting on the serving table, set a beach ball in a towel-lined straw basket. The basket will prevent the ball from rolling. Encourage the guests, before they begin to serve themselves, to write their signatures on the ball. Provide several felt-tip pens in different colors. Make sure there are sufficient white and light-colored surfaces on the ball.

Since graduation is an event where it is customary to look back, set up photo vignettes of the guest-of-honor. One table could have a preschool picture of the graduate and perhaps a favorite toy or blanket. A second table could have an elementary picture along with a group picture of the best friends variety. A third table could hold the junior high picture along with a musical instrument or ball associated with those years. A fourth table could hold memories from the senior high years. These vignettes need only two or three items to make an interesting and personal table setting.

Other Possibilities

🍃 A colorful but useful centerpiece can be something as simple as straw baskets full of snack-size treats. Tie helium-filled balloons around one or two of the snack bags and pile more bags on top, anchoring the balloons and satisfying teenage appetites all at the same time.

🍃 If a decorated cake is the main feature, take the opportunity to flash a message — Perhaps something like "Fly high graduate!"

🍃 Show off that graduation picture by placing it prominently on the buffet table.

Fifty Wedded Years

This grand 50th anniversary demands elegance. Whether formal or casually elegant, the table should reflect the fact that this is more than an everyday dining occasion.

If you want to be terribly formal, you should use gold service plates, sometimes called charger plates. These oversize plates are placed under dinner plates. For a more casually elegant look, skip the service plates and use white plates with a border of gold or another color. An elegant table, whether casual or formal, requires your best china.

Cover the table with white moire draped to the floor. Add splashes of gold metallic sequins to the tabletop and sides. Buy sequins in fabric-backed widths purchased by the yard. Tack the widths on the white moire in a criss cross design. Make sure the sequins won't cross under the place settings; the dinnerware should sit solidly on the table.

An elegant table for this occasion calls for a centerpiece of yellow and gold flowers. The flowers, preferably from your garden or the florist shop, should be arranged simply. Don't aim for symmetry, Simply arrange three or four different shapes and tints of yellow and gold flowers as if they were growing together naturally. Select a gold-edged crystal bowl to hold the flowers. If you prefer a low-priced container, use a plastic, gold-painted saucer with foam. Then be sure to fill in the foam completely with flowers and greenery so the saucer and foam are hidden.

Use a makeshift pedestal to raise the floral centerpiece up so it is not in the guests' line of sight. Any empty can or low, sturdy box will do. Drape the pedestal with a piece of gold moire. Then put it on a circular mirror so you double the value of the flowers from the reflection.

Make use of lights on the table setting. If there are spotlights on the ceiling or walls, arrange them so they showcase the table. Set votes on the mirror around the centerpiece to reflect light on the underside of the centerpiece. Dot the table with more votives to blend the soft light throughout the table.

No fiftieth-anniversary table is finished unless it is replete with pictures. Start with the wedding day pictures of the anniversary couple and work your way through the years of children, grandchildren, and family occasions. Put these pictures in gold frames and set them about the table at strategic points. It's always a help when the names of the people, the occasion of the picture, and year are written next to each picture. Fold a white card in half to make a tent, and write the information in black ink.

Party favors for this event require a special effort. In this case, truffles — rich chocolate candies) — work wonderfully. Shop your better candy store for small gold boxes that hold two truffles. You may have to use the candy maker's box with logo, but the important thing is to find the box. It should be about $2^3/4$ x $1^1/4$ by $1^1/4$ inches deep. Select two different truffles, one light chocolate and one dark.

The next step is to have a printer make up white cards (heavy cover paper) sized to fit in the box on top of the chocolates. Select a Times Roman Bold Italic typeface and have printed:

For the Occasion of
Tom's and Mary's
50th Wedding Anniversary
August 3, 1992

After the cards are printed, paste a strand of gold curly ribbon on the bottom edge of each card. About 12 inches should hang from each end of the card. Curl the ribbon ends tightly before putting the card in the box. Close the cover on the card, with the curly ends hanging from each side outside the box. Set a box of truffles at each place setting.

Other Possibilities

🍂 The floral centerpiece could be made up of the same flowers used for the bridal bouquet fifty years ago.

🍂 Instead of the floral centerpiece, you could arrange to have a replica of the wedding cake at center stage.

On-hand Magic

Starter Sets

Easy to admire, a joy to acquire, quality tabletop appointments give lasting beauty and pleasure. However you choose, start with the minimum of pieces and build your collection from there.

Most people starting households have a hodgepodge of hand-me-downs and mismatched items, but they usually have the basic everyday needs covered. What is needed is a well-thought-out plan to collect quality table appointments. A collection is started with what is often called a starter set.

In the best of all worlds, one has at hand a versatile assortment of select table appointments. However, this is not a possibility and in fact is not really desired. Budget considerations aside, you'll want to allow space and time to develop your taste. Properly selected table appointments take time and thought to acquire.

Most people begin to think seriously about quality tabletop appointments when they plan to wed in the near future. This is largely because of the influence of the wedding registry. Department and tabletop stores offer the registry to soon-to-be-married couples. The couple may list, or register, their choice of dinnerware, silverware, and crystal, as well as other household needs. Friends and relatives have the option of buying tabletop wedding gifts from this list without a lot of speculation about the couple's likes and dislikes.

On the other hand, you don't need to have a wedding to acquire quality table appointments. Anyone can begin at any time to build a lovely and beautiful tabletop collection.

It's not difficult to choose tableware appointments with lasting appeal. Generally speaking, if you buy only what truly sparks your interest, you'll end up with an interesting and put-together tabletop collection. Begin with basic pieces, just as you would with your wardrobe, and highlight with unusual accessories.

Starter sets of dinnerware are made up of place settings that usually include five pieces: dinner plate, salad plate, bread and butter plate, cup, and saucer. You may decide to mix and match. In that case, choose, for example, a dinner plate and cup and saucer in one design, and fill in with a showy or ornate salad plate and bread and butter plate.

It's not necessary, but it is helpful, if you first decide what dinnerware you prefer. Most dinnerware has either an ivory or white tone, so consequently you'll want to color-key your tablecloths and place mats to your dinnerware choice.

Tablecloths run in standard sizes. Of course, you must know your tabletop size. If you haven't acquired a dining table yet, it's helpful to know that most tables are a standard 30-inch or 36-inch round or 42 x 54-inch or 48 x 72-inch oval. Many times leaves can be inserted into a table to increase its surface and accommodate more place settings. You will need one damask tablecloth or a cotton tablecloth handcrafted with embroidery, cutwork or lace. Be sure a table pad is on your list as well. Also add one luncheon cloth in a print or solid color and one set of place mats. With the tablecloths and place mats, include matching or coordinating napkins.

Glassware falls into two categories: tumblers and stemware. Aside from the tumbler, you really need only one basic size of stemmed glass for starters — the 4-ounce wine glass. It can be used for any wine and can also be pressed into service for sherry, champagne, and fruit juice. Goblet and flute stemware are usually the next purchases made.

Sterling silver flatware is sold in four-piece place settings. A place setting includes a teaspoon, place fork, place knife, and salad fork. Stainless steel and silverplate flatware are offered in a five-piece place setting consisting of place fork, place knife, soup spoon, salad fork, and teaspoon. Well-designed stainless steel flatware for everyday use offers carefree quality with the look of sterling.

All the suggested items are basic tableware appointments. Fill-in pieces such as serving pieces, holloware, and crystal should eventually be considered — some pieces sooner than later. It's worth saying one more time: Building a quality tabletop collection takes time and the gradual development of your taste. The satisfaction is in the search and deliberation as well as the actual acquisition.

Effortless Elegance

Elegance at your fingertips. Even though you may not have had time to collect a tabletop wardrobe, you can create a delightful table using items around you in unexpected ways.

It's fair to say that people who haven't devoted their time or budgets to the tabletop still enjoy entertaining every so often. Unfortunately, there may not be a tablecloth to fit the dining table or enough tableware pieces to set an elegant table.

Nevertheless, a beautiful table can still be managed. Lovely items from your clothing wardrobe, room accessories, or items from long-time personal collections await you. What it takes to pull it all together is an eye for possibilities. And, as crazy as it sounds, the pressure of limited resources is often the catalyst to achieving serendipitous results. Sometimes the very fact that you are pressured to make do with things on hand can lead you to end up making a very personal statement.

The table cover suggested here is perhaps the easiest and at the same time the most dramatic solution in this scenario. This is the time to go into your clothes wardrobe. Pull out that seldom-used silk or rayon shawl and spread it out across the center of the table for instant drama. If a shawl isn't available, then turn to your coat scarves, the kind everyone receives as a gift at least once or twice in their adult lifetime. With luck, the scarves are color-coordinated, but if not, a careful and judicious placement of unmatched scarves on the table will turn the tabletop into a kaleidoscope of color.

If you've followed the principle of buying only those things you love, your dishes should provide a lovely counterpoint to the table covering. Very likely the colors you selected for your personal wardrobe are the same colors you chose for your household furnishings, including the dinnerware. Your dinnerware should do very nicely against the shawl or scarf background.

You can make your everyday set of dinner and salad plates, soup bowls, and cups and saucers look new again simply by using them in unexpected ways. For example, rather than using the salad plates to serve the salad course, use them as service plates for stemmed glassware. Use the same duo to serve an appetizer (such as melon balls or seafood cocktail) or dessert (such as ice cream and fresh fruit topping or bread pudding). If used as an appetizer, set the service plate and stemmed glass on the dinner plate. If serving dessert, place the service plate directly on the table.

Coffee cups and saucers can be spruced up, too. Pinch off fresh flower petals from a flowering plant or floral arrangement and lay one or two fresh petals on the saucer next to the cup. This is a small gesture but one that adds freshness to the setting. Details do make a difference.

Turn any plain, undistinguished water glass into a tumbler you can be proud of. Fill the glass to the brim with freshly made ice cubes. Then prepare thin slices of fresh fruit to float in the water or hang over the rim of the glass. Select orange, lemon, or lime, depending on your menu. Tuck a stemmed cherry on top of the ice. Or, add one or two green herbal leaves to the beverage; mint or parsley comes to mind. Be sure to include these items on your grocery list so you won't have to make an extra shopping trip.

There are several possibilities for centerpieces. Inject some personality into a centerpiece of flowers by twining pearl or gold ropes from your jewelry collection around the vase and down about the table. Taking another tack, scout around for any old and forgotton collections you might have. Shell or rock collections are always easy to use on the tabletop. Collections like toy racing cars, miniature boxes, and tiny plush animals can add the flavor you need to finish the table in high style.

Other Possiblities

🍂 An elegantly folded napkin can make an old napkin look new in a special way. See *Folding Table Napkins,* from Brighton Publications, for dozens of ways to fold napkins.

🍂 Move the dining table to an area (in the dining room or another room) where there is directed or controlled lighting to highlight the setting.

Low-cost Romance

Lusting for a romantic white and lace tabletop look, but limited by your budget? Then it's time to be innovative and creative, and look for some inexpensive alternatives.

While a lace linen tablecloth may be out of your price range, pretty white net panel curtains provide a reasonably priced, easily available alternative. Window curtains provide yards of fabric at a much lower price but still give the look of elegance. Buy enough net panel curtains to layer them and swathe the table in generous folds. Drop puddles of curtain from the table to the floor.

Set one or two lace panels aside for an extra touch to the table dressing. After the tablecloth of net has been put in place, swag a lace panel around the edge of the table. At each high point of the swag affix a lace bow. There are wonderful possibilities for the bow. Look for lace eyelet, crochet work, or embroidered organdy lengths on the remnant tables in home decorating departments or stores. If necessary, cut the lengths to size to make the bow.

The same lace pieces used for the table bows can also be used to romance the napkins. Simply tie a length of lace around a plain white cotton napkin. Pinch the center of the opened napkin and shake gently, making sure that the edges of the napkin fall together in loose folds. Then, just a little below where you pinched the napkin, loosely tie the length of lace to hold the napkin folds together. Tie the length in either a loose knot or a bow.

In the center of the table you can arrange a floral centerpiece that will pick up the romantic white and lace theme. First, you won't need a cut glass flower vase. Instead find a clear glass vase. Inexpensive glass containers with interesting shapes can be found in such unlikely spots as the saladware department and in import shops. In the glassware department, you may find oversized goblets or tall cylinder glassware. In some cases you may be able to find an oversize brandy snifter.

Once you have the glass vase in hand, settle a layer of clear glass pebbles or marbles at the bottom. Then arrange an elegant bouquet of white flowers. In-season cut garden flowers are the best value in town. If you're not friends with a gardener, shop your local farmer's market. When in season, select from white tulips, white lilacs, Queen Ann's lace, white roses, white phlox, white daisies, or white chrysanthemums.

For individual centerpieces, cut from the edge of a small round paper doily to the center and remove a small circle. Overlap the cut edges and tuck into a small water glass. Stand a tiny bouquet of garden flowers like white daisies and baby's breath through the paper doily in the water glass.

Avoid setting one candle on each side of the floral centerpiece. Use several candles of the same color on the table. Set the candles in groups or singly, but vary the heights. If you have to, cut tapers to the length you need, or set candles on pedestals to get different heights.

Clear glassware is a good substitute for the china tableware you normally would expect to see in this kind of table setting. Select large, dinner-sized, clear glass plates and use as a service plate (charger). Arrange a round doily on top and then set a luncheon-size plate on top of that. Round doilies can still be found at church sales and at antique or secondhand shops. Sometimes newly made doilies can be found at your local dime store.

Of course, although it shouldn't have to be said, if you have one good table piece to showcase, do so. This can be something as small as an elegant glass paperweight or a set of your grandmothers' silver dessert spoons. Whatever the item, give it a place of honor on this low-budget but high-romance table.

Other Possibilitites

🍂 Before putting the net curtain panels on the table, first dip the net panels in a weak tea solution, then dry. This gives the panels the look of old treasured lace.

🍂 A bobeche (bo beśh) can add more shimmer and shine to the table. This is a small dish of glass or metal with a center hole that sits around the top of a candlestick to catch the candle wax drippings.

Anything Goes

*When the tried and true just won't do ...
put your imagination to work. Use a tired
piece in a new way or adapt a nondining
piece for tabletop use.*

Sometimes the simplicity of design will spark your imagination. At other times, sheer necessity bubbles an idea to the surface. Whatever the source, you'll find when "anything goes" wonderful, beautiful tables can happen.

Table linens are a good example. There are many sources close at hand, some as near as your closet where you can find unique and colorful table coverings and napkins. Consider bandanas, hankerchiefs, and shawls. Or look to other household items such as sheets and pillowcases or terrycloth fingertip towels and washcloths. Remnants in the sales bins of fabric stores are wonderful treasures. Indian blankets or Mexican serapes make a marvelous ethnic background statement. Old crocheted bedspreads suggest a wonderfully romantic table.

Use your napkins, but put them in new places on the place setting. Pop them in glasses or cups, or wind them through coffee mug handles. Use anything but an overused napkin ring to highlight the napkin. Consider bracelets or rings or go to your baking supplies and pull out your decorative cookie cutters. Pile rolled napkins tied with ribbon on a china platter for a buffet presentation.

Use lidded jars to serve jam for a buffet brunch. Pour salad dressings from a gravy boat. Serve vinegar and oil from saki bottles and present tea bags in a wicker basket. Serve condiments or dinner mints and nuts in exquisite stemmed glasses. It's the unexpected that delights your guests and highlights your menu.

Use opened fans for place mats. A different mood is required? Try lacquer trays at each setting for an ultramodern look. Get playful and place finished jigsaw puzzles under the place setting. Select puzzle subjects that tie in with your theme.

Centerpieces are easy. Although floral arrangements are quite beautiful, any number of other ideas can charm and beguile your guests. Try collections of glass paperweights, tin soldiers, electric trains (track and all!), or seashells. Float candles in a lotus bowl or use a dab of clay to hold a candle in a saki cup or stemmed glass. Add glittering glass pieces under the candles to reflect the brilliance doubly. Otherwise draw attention to each place setting with individual centerpieces. Top cruets or tight-lipped bottles with a single stemmed flower. Use ceramic thimbles to hold tiny flowers like violets.

Brush whole nuts with a gold glaze (thinned craft paint) and place a grouping in a small shallow wicker basket. Hollow out round fresh vegetables like artichokes or oranges and fill with flowers and greens.

Paint your china to enhance a theme or personalize a place setting. Decorate egg cups to match the holiday, or write names on coffee mugs to warmly greet your friends. Write your guests' names on napkin rings or porcelain spoon holders for eye-catching name cards. For materials, visit a craft store. You'll need a paint marker or brush and any paint that will work on glass. Most paints are toxic and should be used carefully.

You can see that almost anything can be used to lighten and brighten your table. All it takes is an open look at everything for possibilities. These kinds of unexpected delights can make your table setting one of a kind . . . not a product of a glitzy magazine layout.

Apartment Style

A sit-down-style dinner for six or more in a small apartment requires some skilful planning. Astute use of furniture and tableware creates the sought-after effect.

Because living spaces in apartments are often tight and cramped, dining surfaces are, by necessity, small. Space — any space — is at a premium. Often other furniture pieces must take the place of a formal dining table.

When entertaining in the small apartment, one needs to look at available options to tables. If you have a workroom/study area, there should be a round table, desk, library table, or drafting table that can be used. Simply pull the piece out to the center of the room and set up for dining. Extra chairs you need might be stored throughout the other rooms in the apartment. Buy chairs that can act as occasional chairs, cover them in one color that can work in every room, and distribute them in the living, hall, and bedroom areas.

Lacking those items, set up a portable table such as a card table along with folding chairs. The table and chairs can be stored in a closet or under the bed when not in use.

Setting the table itself is much the same as for any formal table. However, there is one consideration to give to this particular setting — space. Dining for more than two can often present some problems.

In most cases it will be a bit of a squeeze to position more than two or four place settings on a small table or desk. In that event, use a full tablecloth rather than place mats. Since the tablecloth doesn't have natural boundaries for the place setting as place mats do, each space for a place setting can be reduced and extra settings can be arranged on the table, making what appears to be space for four into space for six.

More space can be arranged by giving some thought to placing the napkins at each place setting. Most people simply lay the napkins to the left of the place setting without much thought. Unfortunately, on a small table there isn't enough space for this kind of placement. Rather put the napkin on the plate or above the place setting. If there is a bread-and-butter plate, you can set the napkin on that plate. This may not result in room for another place setting, but at least it will give the appearance of a more spacious table.

Realizing space is tight on the dining table, plan the menu and table setting accordingly. Bread-and-butter plates may take up too much room; three different stemmed glasses at each place setting will do the same. Stick to a simple main course of two or three items. Serve appetizers and dessert away from the table in the living area. Through the dinner, whenever you add dishes to the table, try to take away a like number to keep the table from becoming too cluttered.

A serving cart is convenient for bringing dishes and food from the kitchen area to the table. It's handy, too, to keep the serving dishes on the cart rather than the table, thereby saving space on the center of the table for condiments and a small centerpiece. The cart can be used as an end table when it's not in service for entertaining.

A low storage wall of shelves near the table is useful to set serving dishes during the meal. In fact, you can shove one end of the table close to the wall; giving you a ledge to set a centerpiece on. If you prefer, set the serving pieces on the shelf and hang a favorite picture on the wall, as a kind of centerpiece. That way you'll have more room for dishes. The shelves can be used as a storage area for your table appointments.

Other Possiblities

🍂 Instead of placing the table against a wall, move it to a window. With lots of hanging plants you will create a conservatory effect for your dining experience.

🍂 When the table is too close for comfort to the kitchen area, place a decorative screen between kitchen and table.

🍂 Use lunch-size plates rather than dinner-size plates to give a better overall proportion to the small table.

Impromptu Party

Simplify the task of table setting. When you decide to entertain on the spur of the moment, apply shortcuts and clever solutions to both the menu and the table.

Has anyone *not* decided to invite guests for dinner on the spur of the moment? It happens and it is a wonderful, spontaneous way to entertain. You can easily match your table setting to this happy-go-lucky mood with things you most likely have on hand.

Your first impulse should be to find food to serve quickly. The local deli is a good solution. Takeout Chinese food is another possibility, or perhaps simply an ordered-in pizza. If you were efficient on your last shopping trip, you'll have a cache of cupboard supplies such as canned meats, soups, or pasta.

Once you have decided on an instant menu, you should decide how best to present this last-minute effort. At the least you'll need some type of table covering or place mat, napkins, dinnerware, and a centerpiece.

You're in luck if you have a freshly laundered tablecloth or place mats in the closet. Otherwise you can turn to this simple solution. Spread brightly colored tissue or wrapping paper on a coffee table or sideboard for buffet serving. Set hot pads underneath any warm serving dishes to protect the furniture.

It's not necessary to remove the food from their containers and put in serving dishes. You can use the cardboard containers the food came in if you camouflage them in this delightful way. Wrap foil wrap around the square or round containers and tie a bright metallic curly ribbon around paper and container to keep the foil in place. Set the wrapped containers on a glass round or square. Choose a scheme of two contrasting colors or select a rainbow of colors for the tissue tablecloth and foil-wrapped containers. For example, bright pink and dark purple always make a dramatic statement.

Since there isn't a good way to disquise pizza boxes, you'll have to use a serving dish. The pizza should be placed on as many platters as needed. Then arrange stemmed sherbet glasses of Parmesan cheese in a half-circle behind the tray.

Other quick eye-catching ideas include using fresh food as serving dishes. Serve marinated vegetables or salad in a scooped-out fresh head of cabbage or cauliflower. Use fresh leaves of red leaf or bibb lettuce underneath the cabbage. Fresh loaves of bread from the bakery can be hollowed out and used as serving dishes, too. A round loaf is the right size for the chip or veggie dip; an elongated loaf is good for a variety of cheese cubes and cold cut slices.

A quick centerpiece can be made from any green plant in your home. Wrap the plant's pot using the same foil you used to cover the deli containers. Again use the same metallic curly ribbon to tie and hold the paper around the planter. Use one medium-size plant or arrange a grouping of three 4-inch pots on a tray. Cover the bottom of the tray with pebbles or marbles.

Other Possibilities

❧ Stack in spiral fashion the largest and most colorful paper napkins you can find. Make sure each guest has more than enough.

❧ Serve beverages in your best cups and glasses. The senses will be more than satisfied with the sight, taste, and touch sensations.

❧ If you have some colorful fresh fruit, spread a few about the tissue paper for interest. Small tangerines, kumquats, or bunches of green grapes make a pleasing high-color contrast against a dark shade of tissue paper.

❧ Set the mood with party lighting. If you have a dimmer switch, gradually lower lights over the course of the evening. Use spots or candles to draw attention to the centerpiece.

❧ Quality background music will lift the most hastily conceived get-together into a first-class party.

How-to Basics

Twelve Tips to $ave Tabletop Dollars

❧ Purchase good dinnerware. Build an elegant dinnerware collection gradually. By selecting an open-stock dinnerware pattern, you can purchase pieces at your convenience. Start with two basic place settings and add to the set when possible. Know how long the pattern is guaranteed to be available! Also, ask if the pattern is offered at sale price on occasion.

❧ Go slowly. Don't buy everything at once. Let time and experience shape your likes and dislikes. Then take advantage of sales and special buying opportunities to fill in your table setting beautifully. If you find yourself usually choosing a certain color or design in household furnishings, it's a good sign that you'll enjoy the same color or design for your table setting.

❧ Purchase basic dinner plates that will lend themselves to mix-and-match cups, salad plates, and dessert plates at a later date. The time to indulge in a favorite bright color or pattern is when you're selecting salad or dessert plates. It's easier to replace small plates to change the look of the table setting.

❧ Use eye-catching pieces. Set off a table setting of inexpensive pottery with one or two distinctive pieces. A serving dish, pitcher, or unique serving utensil can make a definite statement. Art museum gift shops, gift catalogs, and craft shows are good sources of unusual pieces.

❧ Make your own linens. If you know a basic hemming stitch, you can sew tablecloths, place mats, and napkins. Check out the dress and drapery remnant tables in fabric stores first. It takes only a small amount of fabric to make four place mats or napkins. Be sure the fabric you select is washable, colorfast, and in the case of napkins, absorbent for easy wiping.

❧ Turn those nights of television into quality time. Crochet edgings, cross-stitch, or appliqué inexpensive linens for an exquisite and romantic tabletop look. Start with small projects to see the fruits of your labor quickly.

❧ Learn a variety of napkin folds to keep the table setting fresh and inviting without having to acquire more tabletop pieces. *Folding Table Napkins* (Brighton Publications), by Sharon Dlugosch, offers stand-alone folds, tuck-in glass folds, napkin ring folds, and special party folds.

❧ Collect tabletop accessories when traveling. This way you'll be sure to enjoy your souvenir for a long time. Napkin rings and flower vases are always good to bring home, but try for more unusual pieces such as seashells that can be used for the base of a centerpiece or as place cards, and ethnic scarves that can be used as place mats or napkins.

❧ Let your kitchen provide inspiration for centerpieces. Fruit and vegetable arrangements reflect a naturally abundant and fresh look. Add green or dried leaves to the base of the arrangement, sprinkle glitter on the fruit or vegetable pieces, or tuck in nuts, still in the shell, here and there in the arrangement.

❧ Don't turn thumbs down on other's outcasts. With a little imagination in arranging, you may be able to set a one-of-a-kind table. And, who knows, ten years from now you'll have a head start on valuable collector's items. Mix and match hand-me-downs to make a complete setting. Next-to-new shops will provide fill-in pieces.

❧ Plan three or four good entertaining menus, keeping in mind the tableware you have on hand. For example, choose hearty but simple dinner menus that can be displayed beautifully with casual country pottery pieces. Try not to include recipes in the menu that will require you to purchase new dishes. Give the same care to determining the size of the food portions. Small portions can look lost on large dinner plates.

❧ Choose decorations that will carry through the seasons. A basic wreath can be used again and again if it's embellished with seasonal ribbons and flowers. The same can be done with a moss-covered topiary or a straw hat. Ask your florist for choosing flowers that are readily available and inexpensive.

Selective Shopping

❧ Plain dishes or those with bands of color or a very simple design allow the most variety in linens. On the other hand, lace, white or plain-color table linens offer a subdued background for exuberantly printed dinnerware.

❧ White china is adaptable to most decorating schemes. Use with crystal and silver on linen or lace for an elegant look; mix with shining black for a high-tech look; set on a background of patterned place mats for a country look; or add to tropical prints for an exotic look.

🐝 Some china companies are now introducing "mix-and-match" patterns. This is in response to the new tabletop trend of mixing patterns and colors. Often the accent plate (also called the accessory salad plate) is embellished with more detailing than the dinner plate and cup and saucer. In some cases, you have a choice of either accent plate or the traditional salad plate to round out the standard five-piece setting.

🐝 It's common practice to select for the wedding registry two sets of dinnerware: fine and casual china. But if space will be at a premium or there will be several moves in the immediate future, it could be a wiser decision to opt for only one set of dinnerware. Select the dinnerware as you would a basic dress — as something that can be accessorized for both formal and informal occasions.

🐝 When choosing glassware, consider these points. The stem of a wine glass should be tall enough so you can hold the glass without touching the bowl. Be aware that hollow-stemmed glasses are harder to clean. Clear glass displays the color and clarity of the wine best.

🐝 Talk to the people behind the silver flatware and holloware counter. Ask if one company's silver seems to need more polishing than another's. They know because they clean the silver week after week.

🐝 Dishes that go from freezer to microwave to dishwasher are time and space savers. One dish performs three functions: storing, cooking, and serving.

Special Care Tips

🐝 Since the weakest point of a glass is around its rim it's best not to set the glass upside down when storing it.

🐝 Although the dishwasher is a wonderful convenience, be aware that putting glassware in the dishwasher over time will result in small scratches etched in the glass. This takes a long time, so the first year or so of dishwashing won't show the scratches, but you can depend on seeing scratches eventually.

🍂 The kitchen sink faucet is a serious hazard for glasses. Breakage often occurs when washing and rinsing. For that reason, put a rubber protector around the tip of the faucet.

🍂 China trimmed with gold needs special handling. Since the gold is applied after the glaze, high temperatures will soften the gold. The china should be washed in the dishwasher at the lowest temperature setting.

🍂 Don't remove china from the dishwasher until it is cool. It is possible to leave a thumbprint on gold softened by heat.

🍂 As with glasses, if the dinnerware is always washed in the dishwasher, you will notice a wearing of the gold after several years of use around ten to fifteen years.

🍂 Some consideration has to be given before putting flatware in the dishwasher, too. When sterling silver and stainless steel are washed in the dishwasher at the same time, a chemical reaction occurs that can result in pitting of the sterling silver. Because knives are made up of sterling silver handles and stainless steel blades (sterling silver is too soft to use for cutting), they should not be washed in the dishwasher.

🍂 Sterling silver forks and spoons can be washed in the dishwasher, but only if you don't include your metal pots and pans.

🍂 Never soak your table knives, because of the joint between the blade and handle. Water can get into the joint and can literally swell the joint to the point of exploding.

🍂 Test your china in the microwave. If the dish gets hot, it means there is some metal in the clay from which it was made. Using the dish in the microwave may cause damage to the dish.

🍂 Always have something between your china pieces when storing them. A piece of felt or the plastic bubble sheeting found in packing boxes works well.

🍂 Antique tablecloths and other fine linens should be washed in hot water. Use laundry soap and a small amount of chlorine bleach. Hand-wash and then place items in the spin cycle of the washing machine to get all the water out. Don't put finer items like lace or fine cottons in the spin cycle.

Quick Tricks

- Keep tablecloths rolled so they don't have to be ironed before covering the table. This saves wear and tear on your fine linens as well because you won't always fold on the same crease.

- Store place mats flat and napkins folded simply into fourths.

- Keep a supply of different colored or printed paper napkins on hand just in case your fabric napkins are in the laundry when you want to set the table.

- Clutter seems to accumulate on the table as naturally as bees are attracted to honey. Try to keep the tables cleared and 50 percent of your time will be saved.

- Choose white or ivory tableware so that you can easily coordinate with any color, whether linens, centerpiece, or candles.

- Brush up on table setting and serving skills so you don't have to stop to figure it all out when you're in a hurry.

- Set the table only with pieces your menu will require. For example, don't add a dessert spoon to the place setting if dessert will be served in the living room or not at all.

- Have centerpiece supplies at hand. If storage is at a premium, at least have one or two favorite flower vases, a plastic saucer, a brick of florist foam, florist tape, and a sharp knife available.

- Store an evening's worth of candles in the freezer. Candles burn more slowly and evenly once they're chilled.

- Collect reference handbooks as you do cookbooks. Such titles as *Folding Table Napkins* and *Table Setting Guide* (Brighton Publications, Inc.) can give you design possibilities as well as nuts and bolts information quickly at your fingertips.

- Do as much as possible ahead of time. If the table is set the day before, you may need to drape clean towels or a sheet over the table to keep the dust off.

- Keep a record of your biggest tabletop triumphs. Make a list of guests attending. Then when you entertain a new set of friends, you'll have a clear-cut record to follow.

- Tie ribbons around candles and napkins for a festive look.

❧ Pick up fresh flowers or plants at the same place you buy the menu ingredients.

Fresh Flower Arrangement

Here is how to create quick and easy fresh flower arrangements that utilize an appropriate container blending with or highlighting your table setting.

❧ You'll need a florist foam brick, florist tape, a metal container such as a bread pan or a plastic saucer, and a sharp knife.

❧ Purchase from your florist a sturdy green plant material such as leather leaf, Italian ruscus, or myrtle to hide the foam brick and the flower stems.

❧ If the foam brick is too large for the plastic saucer, cut it in half. It will extend well above the saucer's lip. A whole foam brick will fit in a rectangular loaf pan if laid on its side. It should extend about 1 inch from the top.

❧ Cut the stems of the flowers on the diagonal and condition them in warm water up to an hour or overnight.

❧ With the florist tape, tape the foam crosswise securely to the container. Cover with green plant material to hide the foam.

❧ Add the flowers, inserting through the green plant material and extending 2 inches into the foam. Start at the center and fill in, letting the lower flowers extend over the edges.

❧ Set the saucer or bread pan into the decorative container. If necessary, raise the flower arrangement by setting it on a brick or block of wood. The edge of the pan or saucer should be even with the top of the outer container.

❧ Add water until the foam is completely soaked.

Easy Centerpieces

❧ Scrunch together small mesh wire netting and tuck it into a wide shallow container — for example, a vegetable serving dish. Select flowers with harmonizing colors. If you're not comfortable selecting colors that work together, then choose tones of one color. Select flowers for their variety in texture and shape as well as color.

❀ Wrap a large dinner-sized fabric napkin around a squat empty jar. Choose a bright, party pattern. Set the jar in the center, pull up the ends, and gather the napkin around the top of the jar. Use a ribbon to hold the napkin in place. Arrange lightweight flowers such as baby's breath or violet. A set of three will give optimum impact.

❀ Hollow out artichokes, fill with water, and pop in some white flowers with a few green leaves. White daisies, Queen Ann's lace, or white Gerbera are possibilities. For drama, try one white lily blossom. Cut stem close to the head.

❀ Individual centerpieces, alone or as an accessory to the major centerpiece, add eye-beckoning appeal. Try green pears with a magnolia leaf or any other broad leaf stuck jauntily at the top. Splash the magnolia leaves with gold paint. Need name tags? Write each guest's name with a felt-tip pen on a gold leaf.

❀ Flowers and fruit, such as green grapes and rosebuds, combine beautifully in a glass-stemmed compote dish. Select rosebuds in warm apricot tones. Remember, this arrangement will last only for a few hours, since the rosebuds are tucked in among the grapes and don't have their stems in water.

❀ Floating candles in a wide shallow bowl make their own romantic statement. Sprinkle a few rose or hibiscus blossoms on the water as a counterpoint to the candles. Candle and blossom color should blend for soft eye appeal.

❀ Group a cluster of five to eight champagne flutes on the center of the table or march the flutes in a single line down the center of the table. Each glass should sport a single stemmed flower spray. Consider small flower orchids or dendrobiums.

❀ An arrangement of small deep red roses and purple statice warms a wintry day. Use a shallow round glass bowl, flower vase, or sugar bowl as the container. Purchase enough rose stems so that the mouth of the bowl holds the bouquet tightly. Then there will be no need for a foam brick. Cut the stems so that the rose blossoms stand just above the mouth of the bowl, mounded gently. Tuck in the purple statice between the roses.

For different occasions use other colors. For example, substitute coral roses and yellow statice for a Mexican fiesta theme.

🌿 Any flower or bouquet of flowers can be set off with an on-hand tabletop piece. Here is a list of possibilities: egg cups, tiny glass tumblers, stemmed glassware, sugar bowls, candy dishes, vinegar cruets, soup plates, delicately painted china cups, coffee mugs, pitchers, and shallow reed baskets.

Making Cut Flowers Last

🌿 Always put cut flowers into water right away. Water is as necessary to flowers as air is to us.

🌿 Use a knife to cut stems of flowers. Use pruning shears to cut roses and other woody stems.

🌿 Cut roses under water with pruning shears so the flower will suck the water up to its head. If you don't, the rose stem will callus over and prevent the water from reaching all the way to the head of the flower. Then plunge the stem in warm water. There is a method to revive roses with drooping heads: Recut the stem under warm water and wait for about an hour. If the bud doesn't stand straight, repeat the process again. Some woody stems like lilacs are best cut under water, too.

🌿 Recut rose stems $1/8$ to $1/4$ inch each day or every other day. The stems can only absorb so much water every day before they callus over.

🌿 Commercial floral preservative, cool room temperature, and water are the three key ingredients to extending the vase life of flowers. Adding water or changing the water frequently is also paramount to a long-lasting bouquet.

🌿 Strip leaves that fall below the waterline from stems. Leaves in the water create more bacteria, resulting in clogged stems.

🌿 Any flower vase, including bud vases, should be washed and-bleached if necessary. Otherwise, the bacteria will continue to grow, even in fresh water.

🌿 Keep flowers in a cool spot, refrigerator or basement, until a few hours before showtime. The cool temperature will extend the life of the flowers.

❧ Pinch unopened gladioli buds off at the top of the spray. The buds at the top get the water first, so if they are pinched the flowers that are left will retain their color and live longer.

❧ Pull the stamen off lilies such as the tiger lily or Easter lily. The flower will live longer and won't be as messy. If brushed against clothing, the lily stamen can leave a stain.

❧ When cutting spring bulb flowers, set the daffodil aside in a separate pail of water for about 10 minutes. This will allow the gooey mixture flowing from the daffodil stem to run out into the water. The gooey mixture contains a substance that harms the other cut flowers.

❧ By pinching off the little mouth or nose of the orchid, you may extend its life. The orchid is long-lived anyway so this may not really make a difference.

❧ Garden iris are an exception to the rule of adding a commercial floral preservative to the water. The iris will begin to droop and wilt in a matter of hours if put in water into which a preservative has been added. Woody stem flowers need a special preservative.

❧ By now you're wondering what is considered an extended life for a bouquet. You've done well if the bouquet lasts a week. Of course, the flower you're working with does make a difference.

Sewing Table Linens

❧ For tablecloth yardage, figure the size of the tablecloth plus a 10-inch overhang and a 1-inch hem. The tablecloth should end approximately 2 inches above the chair seat.

❧ For the width of an oblong or oval tablecloth, add the width of the table (at widest point for an oval table), plus twice the overhang, plus enough fabric to turn up a 1-inch hem. Divide this figure by the width of your fabric.

❧ To find the length of the table, measure the table length, plus twice the overhang, plus the 1-inch hem. Multiply the widths by the lengths to give you the total yardage needed.

❧ To figure yardage for round tablecloths, add the diameter of the table to the overhang (from 10 inches to the floor) twice, plus the hem. Divide the diameter by the width of the fabric to find how many lengths you will need.

❧ Look at the yardage chart to discover how much fabric you need, depending upon the size of the table and the width of the fabric. This chart assumes all tables are 29 inches high and that fabric is solid-color or an all-over pattern that doesn't have to be matched. In all sizes given, the hemmed edge will be ½ inch from the floor. Adjust for 10-inch overhangs.

Yardage Chart for Round & Oval Tablecloths

Size of Table	Size of Cloth before Hemming	Yards Required				No. of Lengths Required				Length Should Be Cut
		36"	45"	48"	54"	36"	45"	48"	54"	
30" round	89" diam.	7.5	5	5	5	3	2	2	2	90"
36" round	95" diam.	8	8	5.5	5.5	3	3	2	2	96"
48" round	107" diam.	9	9	9	6	3	3	3	2	108"
54" round	113" diam.	9.5	9.5	9.5	9.5	3	3	3	3	114"
60" round	119" diam.	13.25	10	10	10	4	3	3	3	120"
42" x 54" oval	101" x 113"	9.5	9.5	9.5	6.5	3	3	3	2	114"
48" x 72" oval	107" x 131"	11	11	11	7.5	3	3	3	2	132"

❧ Cut the number of lengths required. To avoid a seam running across the center of the cloth, seam one-half width to each side of a full width. The seams will fall near the edge of the table or in the overhang. Three lengths — seam the three full widths together evenly.

❧ To cut round tablecloths, fold seamed fabric in half and then in half again to form a square four layers thick. Pin layers together. Tie a knot around a stick pin at one end of string and secure it to the corner where folded edges meet. Place knot at point of cutting arc. This can either be the finished length of the tablecloth (finish off with a satin stitch) or allow one extra inch for the hem.

❧ Before sewing, prewash the fabric. When stitching seams, place right sides of fabric widths together, with selvedges even. Stitch ½ inch from edge unless deeper seams are necessary (when color or pattern of fabric does not reach to selvedges). Clip selvages at intervals, so seam doesn't pucker. Press seam open.

- 🍂 Finish tablecloth with a 1-inch hem, satin stitching, or applied border (ruffles, lace, or fringe).

- 🍂 For a quick hemming solution, use iron-on tape much as you would shorten your skirt length to hem the tablecloth.

- 🍂 Finished place mats should be 16 to 18 inches long and 12 to 14 inches deep. Cut four rectangular place mats from $3/4$ yard; six rectangular place mats from 1 yard to $1\frac{1}{8}$ yard. Cut four oval place mats from $7/8$ yard and six oval place mats from $1\frac{1}{8}$ yard.

- 🍂 Four pocket place mats require four rectangles $6\frac{1}{2}$ by 5 inches. Press under $\frac{1}{2}$ inch on each side. Turn under $\frac{1}{4}$ inch of raw edge and stitch. Place pocket $\frac{1}{2}$ inch from the left edge and $1\frac{1}{4}$ inch from the bottom of the place mat. Topstitch two sides and bottom in place.

- 🍂 Finish place mats with a zigzag stitch and fringe, a 1-inch hem, or an applied border (such as ruffles or lace).

- 🍂 For fabric required for a table runner, figure 15 to 18 inches wide, the length of the table plus 10 inches overhang at each end. Use 18-inch width to match place mats, 15-inch width if the runner is used alone.

- 🍂 To finish the table runner, hem all four sides or hem the sides and finish the ends with tassels, lace, or fringe.

- 🍂 Napkins sizes vary. Dinner size are 18 to 23 inches square. Luncheon napkins are about 15 to 17 inches square (no smaller than 15 inches). Tea napkins are 12 inches. Cocktail napkins are 4 by 6 inches.

- 🍂 One yard of 45-inch fabric will give four 18-inch napkins.

- 🍂 Lapkins are oversize napkins spread across the lap. Cut a piece of fabric 22 by 26 inches. Finish off the same as napkins.

- 🍂 There are many ways to finish napkin edges. Hem, serge or overlock, fringe (us a zigzag stitch first), crochet edge, and lace are some choices.

Appliqué Method

- 🍂 Purchase paper-backed fusible web (found in most craft stores) in sheets rather than tape rolls for decorative projects. Tape rolls in $3/4$-inch width are available for quick hemming jobs. Check to see if it is machine washable or dry cleanable.

🦋 Fusible web should bond to most fabrics, but always pretest on a scrap of fabric before starting a project.

🦋 Position the textured (rough) side of the fusible web against the wrong side of material. Press for several seconds with a hot (wool setting), dry iron. Let material cool.

🦋 Trace desired pattern onto the fusible web backing sheet, then trim material following the pattern. If you are using a flower from a printed material, simply cut around the flower on the right side of the material.

🦋 To "fuse," cut pattern to desired surface, carefully peel off the paper backing, place fusible side down on desired surface, and cover with a damp pressing cloth and press for approximately 10 seconds with a hot (wool setting), dry iron.

🦋 For large project areas, apply fusible web one section at a time, slightly overlapping until fusible web has been applied to desired area of fabric.

🦋 To keep edges from fraying because of frequent washing, paint around the edge of the cut-out. Use a fabric paint. Brush the paint (again using the rose as an example) onto the inner petals as well so that the paint will seem an integral part of the design. Remember to brush the fabric paint on the right side of the material and before you cut out the design.

🦋 Use for decorating tablecloths, place mats, and napkins.

🦋 Use a hot iron (wool setting) to quickly hem table linens or to create a contrasting edging. Use the $3/4$-inch tape roll.

Stenciling Hints

🦋 It's best for beginners to buy ready-made, precut designs, although you can make your own designs. You'll need a stencil card (found at art or craft supply stores), a sharp knife, and a hard cutting surface. Sketch a design and draw it on the card with a pencil. An alternative is to transfer a pattern onto the card. Once you're satisfied with the pattern, cut out the design with a sharp knife.

🍂 To reproduce the pattern, use specially formulated stencil paint (no more than four different colors are suggested), stencil crayons, or spray paints free of fluorocarbons.

🍂 If paint is your choice, you'll need brushes solely designed for stenciling. They come in different sizes and you must specify whether you'll use them for fabric or hard surfaces.

🍂 Stenciling shows off best on a table surface painted with two or more shades of the same color. Paint the table surface first with one shade of latex paint, sand down with fine sandpaper, apply a second coat in a lighter or darker shade, and sand once again. Top with a varnish or gloss protector.

🍂 Stenciling can be applied directly to an unpainted wooden surface. Clean the surface with soap and water and let dry completely before starting the project.

🍂 Measure the table surface and decide exactly where the stencil should be placed. When cutting the stencil, it helps if the edge of the stenciling card is placed at exactly the table edge. This way, each stencil is the same distance from the edge.

🍂 Dip the tip of the brush in the paint, then work off almost all the paint on a paper towel. If there is too much paint on the brush, the paint will bleed underneath the edges of the stencil card. If the brush is too dry, the design will not appear clearly.

🍂 To paint, hold the brush like a pencil and brush with a circular motion. Start at outer edges and work inwards.

🍂 After paint has dried, give the table surface a good polish to give the surface a mellow look.

🍂 To stencil a tablecloth, use fabric paints or a permanent spray paint. Most spray paints are permanent.

🍂 If using a spray paint, make very sure that the complete cloth is covered. The spray mist may be too fine to see in the air, but it will show up on the cloth, so cover it completely.

Index

Sharon Dlugosch, free-lance home economist, is the author of several books including the best selling *Folding Table Napkins* and *Table Setting Guide.* She has also written several wedding and baby shower books and how-to wedding books. Dlugosch has been conducting tabletop workshops and demonstrations for over fifteen years and continues to create new table settings in her homes in St. Paul, Minnesota and Tucson, Arizona.

Available from
Brighton Publications, Inc.

Folding Table Napkins: A New Look at a Traditional Craft by Sharon Dlugosch

Table Setting Guide by Sharon Dlugosch

Tabletop Vignettes by Sharon Dlugosch

Don't Slurp Your Soup: A Basic Guide to Business Etiquette by Betty Craig

Wedding Plans: 50 Unique Themes for the Wedding of Your Dreams by Sharon Dlugosch

Wedding Hints & Reminders by Sharon Dlugosch

Wedding Occasions: 101 New Party Themes for Wedding Showers, Rehearsal Dinners, Engagement Parties, and More! by Cynthia Lueck Sowden

Games for Wedding Shower Fun by Sharon Dlugosch, Florence Nelson

Baby Shower Fun by Sharon Dlugosch

Games for Baby Shower Fun by Sharon Dlugosch

These books are available in selected stores and catalogs. If you're having trouble finding them in your area send a self-addressed, stamped business-size envelope and request ordering information from:

Brighton Publications, Inc.
P.O. Box 120706
St. Paul, MN 55112-0706